I Love Me 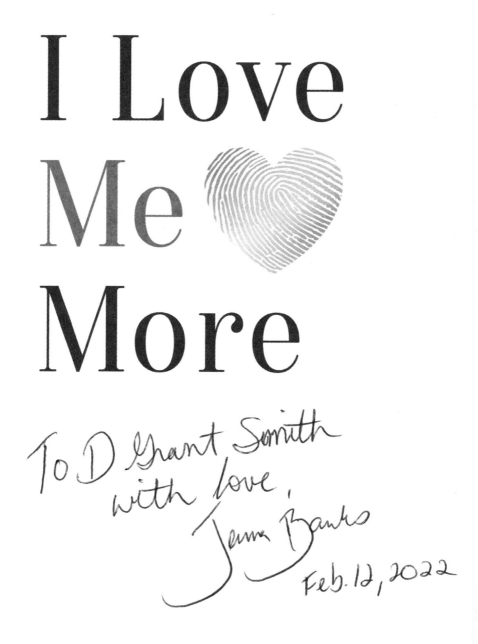 More

To D Grant Smith
with love,

Jenna Banks

Feb. 12, 2022

I Love Me  More

HOW TO FIND HAPPINESS AND SUCCESS THROUGH SELF-LOVE

JENNA BANKS

BrainTrust
INK

BrainTrust Ink
Nashville, Tennessee
www.braintrustink.com

This work is being published under the BrainTrust Ink imprint by an exclusive arrangement with BrainTrust. BrainTrust Ink and the BrainTrust logos are registered trademarks of BrainTrust. The BrainTrust Ink logo is a wholly owned trademark of BrainTrust.

Distributed by Greenleaf Book Group

For ordering information or special discounts for bulk purchases, please contact Greenleaf Book Group at PO Box 91869, Austin, TX 78709, 512.891.6100.

Design and composition by Greenleaf Book Group and Kimberly Lance
Cover design by Greenleaf Book Group and Kimberly Lance

Publisher's Cataloging-in-Publication data is available.

Print ISBN: 978-1-956072-00-6

eBook ISBN: 978-1-956072-01-3

Part of the Tree Neutral® program, which offsets the number of trees consumed in the production and printing of this book by taking proactive steps, such as planting trees in direct proportion to the number of trees used: www.treeneutral.com

TreeNeutral

Printed in the United States of America on acid-free paper

21 22 23 24 25 26   10 9 8 7 6 5 4 3 2 1

First Edition

To every woman out there
who wasn't raised knowing
the concepts of self-love,
every woman who believes,
like I once did,
that true love can only be
found outside herself

CONTENTS

Introduction

My Name Is Jenna, and I'm in Love with Me! (It Wasn't Always This Way)

Love yourself first and everything else falls into line. You really
have to love yourself to get anything done in this world.
—**Attributed to Lucille Ball**

know what it's like to be a powerless child sitting alone in a room waiting to get spanked with a wooden two-by-four. I know what it's like
growing up in household where decisions aren't based on the best interests of the children. I know what it's like to come home from school to
find every dish in the house broken on the floor because of someone's
drunken rage directed at me. I know what it's like to be a teenager who
allows her body to be used by older boys. I know what it's like to be a
grown woman reading abusive words written by a parent. I know what
it's like to attempt suicide because life is so painful and tomorrow and
next week seem like they will be just as bad as today.

I know what it's like to be shaped by these experiences into believing I had no value. I know what it's like to *not* believe in my self-worth,
to *not* let self-respect shape my decisions and actions.

Through hard work and dedication, I have completely changed that
formula. I have become a person capable of self-love. I now know what

it's like to stand up for myself, to set boundaries. To understand that I alone am in control of my state of happiness. I now know what it's like to believe that I have value as a human being, and to base my actions and decisions on respect for myself. I know what it's like to ask for what I want out of relationships.

It's been a long journey, but well worth the effort.

Oddly, it seems to me that self-love is not something we are born with but rather something we must work toward. It is a practice; it is a verb, a constant doing. Self-love is something you choose on a daily basis and often goes against what society and the people around you are pressuring you to do. It's not an addition, a booster, or a supplement. It is the source of all things, of power and energy and of harnessing instead of being harnessed. We must make self-love a lifestyle choice if we are to become truly empowered.

Self-love should feel unconscious, but believe me—there will be many times when you will have to actively and consciously choose to love yourself in order to keep your power your own. We are tested more than we are not, and self-love must be activated and practiced to navigate the challenges, pass those tests, and keep our power. The most active engagement with self-love I've had thus far in my life's journey happened when I ended my relationship with a man named Dave.

The Myth That Self-Love Is Selfish

"Isn't self-love just being selfish?" That's a question I hear a lot when I talk about self-love. Society seems to teach women especially that if we are not giving away our power and energy, if we make decisions based on what will make us happy, then we are being selfish. Nothing could be further from the truth.

A selfish person does not consider the feelings or needs of other people. Their immediate needs are all that matter.

By contrast, someone who practices self-love is aware of the needs of people around them but gives their own needs priority. In fact, it is by loving themselves more that they are able to give more to others. (You'll find more about this issue of selfishness versus self-love in Chapter 2.)

I Love Me More

I had never felt so in love with anyone in all my life as I did with Dave. He and I were the model of passionate love for many of our friends, a barometer that others used to measure what they wanted and were looking for in a relationship. Given his line of work, and our very large group of mutual friends, we were always going on fun adventures, throwing dinners and parties, traveling, and attending events. We were both creative and could take on creative projects together, inspiring each other collaboratively. When Dave and I met we already had children and prior relationships of our own. Well into my adulthood and reaping the wisdom from my experiences, I knew what I needed in a relationship, and I thought I would spend the rest of my life with Dave. I thought of him as my life partner, so helping him with his business, his house, his kids, all came naturally and easily to me.

Shortly after we moved in together, I started feeling off, like I didn't have my usual upbeat energy. I was in the process of ramping up a brand-new business venture, but I found it very difficult to focus on my business. And the affection and passion (and sex) that we had before moving in together fizzled out pretty quickly after we moved in together.

I remember there was a moment after I had been helping all day to get his house ready for sale: scrubbing floors with bleach, patching and painting walls, deep-cleaning bathrooms. At the end of the day, I was completely worn out. He hugged and kissed me, saying, "Thank you, Jenna, for your help. I was feeling so overwhelmed, but now I see the light at the end of the tunnel."

Wow! I thought. *After months of hardly any affection initiated by him, this is what it takes to get some recognition and appreciation?*

But I was so in love that I just carried on, overlooking moments like those that should have been clearer warning signs to me. Luckily for me, I had learned to be tuned in to my instincts. When I don't pick up on subtle clues, my instinct screams at me. Generally speaking, I had been feeling bad, drained of energy, not happy for weeks. I didn't know what I needed but I knew Dave wouldn't be able to give it to me. *Get out. Figure it out later.* This became my constant thought. I couldn't explain in words why I needed to end it, but as you will see throughout this book, if you have the courage to act on the energy that is speaking to you, the words will come later.

I had to break my own heart to do what was best for me. But I knew in the end this man was not capable of valuing me. Either he wasn't wired that way or he didn't want to try. He claimed the former. I could either settle for that and be the giver to a taker, or save me, my power, and my spirit.

Yes, I loved Dave; I loved him madly. *But I loved me more.* So, with much heartache, I broke it off.

Learning to Value Yourself

> When I loved myself enough, I began leaving whatever wasn't healthy. This meant people, jobs, my own beliefs and habits—anything that kept me small. My judgment called it disloyal. Now I see it as self-loving.
>
> —Kim McMillen, *When I Loved Myself Enough*

Not too long after breaking up with Dave, I went to dinner with my friend Emily. She told me she just couldn't understand why I would break up with someone that she knew I was deeply in love with. I told her I broke up with him because "I love me more." She asked me to explain what this meant. So I explained to her some of the self-love concepts I had come to learn over my lifetime that had gotten me to that point. At first, she just couldn't understand this idea at all. It was completely foreign to her. But then, after much contemplation, many weeks later, it finally clicked.

She had been in a tumultuous relationship and wasn't feeling valued by her boyfriend; nor was she getting what she needed from the relationship. She found herself constantly contemplating the relationship and agonizing over it.

One day, she realized something wasn't right, and she connected to my explanation of "I love me more." Suddenly she realized that by accepting how badly her boyfriend had been treating her, *she* hadn't been valuing *herself*. My story gave her the inspiration that she needed to love herself more and choose herself and her happiness over him. She is my inspiration for writing this book.

Living Up to Your Potential

If you have come to this book, you might be as experienced as I am, or even more so, with people taking your power from you, stealing your energy, and using it against you to devalue you and control you. But somewhere you are in tune with your gut, which is telling you there is much more to gain when you learn to love yourself more. And you are right!

In addition to all the emotional and spiritual benefits such as being whole, fulfilled, feeling loved, and being in a state of happiness and joy, there are practical benefits to self-love. In my life, practicing self-love has allowed me to overcome a traumatic childhood and young adulthood. I was able to move up the corporate ladder with just a GED, navigate single parenthood, and negotiate profitable real estate investments. I founded, scaled, and sold my marketing products company, and I leveled up my skill set, my potential, and my relationships.

If I hadn't loved myself more over the past twenty years, I am pretty sure I'd still be working for "the man," living in the same run-down, rent-controlled apartment I'd lived in for seventeen years, with no financial freedom and certainly no opportunity to write this book and share with you what I now know, which is this: We must learn to put ourselves first and know that in doing so, we're not being selfish. Practicing self-love and putting yourself above all others will benefit everyone around you because you will be happier and more at peace. You will create beautiful energy that will benefit the world. You will know true love, a love that can only be found within, and therefore be able to give real love to others.

In addition to all the emotional and spiritual benefits such as being whole, fulfilled, feeling loved, and being in a state of happiness and joy, there are practical benefits to self-love.

All the concepts in this book I've had to figure out on my own or discover through lots of research. My own traumatic family history forced me to become independent very early on in life to survive—and survive not just as a victim but as someone who thrives despite the lack of support or a normal family life. I hope that my personal discoveries captured in this book will help inspire you to go on a journey inward, where true love and security exist. Through this book I want to help you learn to embrace your power and value and create more joy in your life. To help maintain the privacy of the individuals mentioned in my personal stories, some names have been changed.

Part I explains what it means to love yourself and the benefits you will see in your life from doing so. Part II explores all the ways that people—especially women—sabotage themselves because they don't recognize or behave in ways that reflect their true worth. Part III talks about what it means to put yourself first and how challenging it can be. Part IV shows how the inability to love and value ourselves limits what many women achieve in both the workplace and in business, and how you can change that dynamic. Part V addresses one of the biggest struggles we all face: how to find a balance between caring for ourselves and caring for others, be they parents, children, or friends. Part VI has a game plan for specific steps you can take to start reclaiming your value as you learn to love yourself more.

Journaling to Build a Better Relationship with Yourself

When we are in a relationship with someone else—be it a spouse, partner, child, friend, or coworker—we know we need to spend time building and nourishing that relationship. If we want to strengthen a relationship with another person, we're told, "Talk to them. Listen. Be open. Be honest." We're told to check in with them regularly and keep the lines of communication open.

But what do we do to build our relationship with ourselves, which is the most important relationship in our lives?

If we have some deep stuff to work through, we might see a therapist. Or we could seek help from a life coach. But access to therapists and coaches is often limited by availability, money, or time. We could meditate, which is a great way to tune in to yourself regularly. But many folks find this practice too difficult to maintain and end up throwing the idea out the window or just don't practice it on a regular basis. (I do recommend meditating on a daily basis, though; even if you can only squeeze in ten minutes, it's worth it.)

One of the best ways I've found to get to know myself better is through a daily journaling practice. For people who knew me in my younger years, this may sound odd because I used to think that journaling was something like a "Dear Diary" practiced by teen girls. And so the thought of doing it myself never entered my mind.

What got me started on the path to journaling was my desire to open up my creative writing abilities. I'd never considered myself a writer, and so I was looking for something that could help me in this area. But little did I know that journaling would also be an amazing way for me to connect with myself on an intimate level. I had read somewhere that having a daily journaling practice, where you don't edit yourself or overthink what you write, is a great way to get into the flow of writing. The key is to handwrite at least three pages a day and just write anything that comes to mind. The reason for writing by hand is that it slows down the brain, allowing you to better process things.

And so I made a commitment to write at least three pages as part of my morning routine. To my surprise, not only did the practice of journaling allow me to open up the flow of writing; it also helped me work through personal problems and helped me better tune in to myself.

Now, even though I don't feel like I need the practice to help me open up my writing flow anymore, I've kept this as my morning routine because I really love connecting with myself in this way. And if I do skip some days, I really miss that personal connection time.

Even if you've never tried journaling before, I'd like to encourage you to pick up a journal and give it a try. It will make your takeaways from this book so much more impactful and personal. To help you get started, I've included suggested journaling topics for many of the chapters in the hope that they will help you think about what you have, want, and expect from your life. Through a regular journaling practice, you'll get to experience some of the incredible benefits that come with connecting with yourself and knowing yourself better.

Taking a Leap of Faith

Learning self-love is a leap of faith, to say the least. As easily as the words slide off the tongue, self-love is entangled with and entrenched in a whole bunch of other practices, ideas, and truths, making it complex, multilayered, and almost too elusive to grasp. I mean, what does it actually mean to have self-love, and more important, what prevents or thwarts it in the first place?

For a good part of this book, I take you in search of answers to such questions. I elaborate on the stories of my life, like the ones I have touched on in this chapter. Breaking open my inner wounds has allowed me to find the lessons within, and I share them with you through the experiences of my life—the choices I made in response to those people who fill my life, for better or worse.

Whether we are aware of it or not, we harness an abundance of energy—the energy that surrounds us. This is the energy of our thoughts, which govern our emotions. When we "harness" this energy, this means we "control and make use of" it. We can essentially learn to control and use our own energy to our benefit. But you may consider another definition, in which "harness" is a noun, describing a device that is fitted onto something to control it. Our energy can be used by us or taken by others and used against us, and for much of my life, I have experienced the latter. People took my energy, my power source, from me, until I learned how to love myself. How to make that switch is what this book is all about.

I am humbled to the point of tears as I write this introduction, as this book is the result of an arduous internal battle. From abused little girl to a self-made and successful entrepreneur, I am evidence of the power of self-love, of loving oneself more than anyone or anything. I have gone from the deepest, darkest days, hating my life to the point where I would rather die, to the clarity of knowing each day of life is a gift worth fighting to live to the fullest, without shame or guilt, unabashedly and unapologetically releasing the harness of powerlessness to proclaim, "I love me more."

It is my truest hope that whatever you take from this book, whether it be one line, one story, or one fact quoted from a cited expert, you will close the book not with knowledge, but with a feeling—the kind that makes your gut do somersaults—that is telling you somehow you are in the right place, doing the right thing, making the right choice. That choice? You.

PART I

What Is Self-Love?

Self-love. It's not a hard word to define. In fact, if I asked any of my friends, "Can you define self-love?" I bet 100 percent of them would get it right. We know what "self" is, and we know what "love" is, so putting the two together doesn't take a genius: Self-love is when you love yourself.

True. But what I've learned over time is that defining words and understanding their meaning are two very different things. The meaning of the words "self" and "love" is self-evident, but "self-love" as a guiding principle and practice? What does it *mean* to love yourself? Ah, now it just got a little more complex. What does it look like when you love yourself? How is it practiced? And more importantly, why should you care? Those are the questions I explore in this part of the book.

Chapter 1 describes my journey to self-love. I had a difficult childhood, and it has been a long journey to get to a point where I know how to value myself as much as or even more than I value others. As I mention in the introduction, self-love is often confused with selfishness, vanity, or narcissism, but in fact it is the opposite. In Chapter 2, I explore what self-love means. Chapter 3 discusses how self-love can energize us to achieve more than we ever thought possible. In Chapter 4, I explain how learning to monitor your energy is an important skill for practicing self-love.

Chapter 1

My Journey to Self-Love

I came to live the philosophy of loving myself more by first experiencing a life where I had no love in my heart for myself. For many years, I did not know how valuable I was; nor did I realize that I had power over my life and over my reason for living.

I grew up in a family devoted to the Pentecostal faith where you questioned nothing and took the word in the Bible literally. Power and energy were not something inside us, but outside of us, in a wrathful God, in a God to be feared. Watching *Scooby Doo* cartoons warranted prayers of forgiveness, because ghosts were sometimes featured, and, in my family, the only ghost acknowledged as nondemonic (not devil-like) was the Holy Ghost. At nighttime, I would pray for forgiveness of my sins in the event I may have borne witness that day to something or someone sinful. I was raised to believe I was a sinner by simply being around a sinner, as if sin were a contagion. Life was a burden to carry, not a joy to be experienced.

My mother and father divorced when I was just a toddler. My father remarried and had four more children, and I was raised by him and my stepmother in a very strict household. For as far back as I can remember, my stepmother routinely made me sit in my room and read the Bible for hours until my father returned home from work. He would then visit my room and punish me for doing something kidlike: spitting on my half-brother because he spit on me, disobeying a rule such as watching a non-Christian television show or movie at a friend's house, telling a lie, not sharing with a sibling, or even just eating candy (which we weren't allowed to do).

During those years, we were very poor. My stepmom had to use coupons for most everything we purchased. Sometimes we needed to rely on donations from the church for groceries to feed our family of seven. On lucky days, all five of us kids were able to share a single Slurpee from the 7-Eleven convenience store. We also moved around a lot—well over twenty times before I reached age twelve. I was always the new kid in school.

By the time I was fourteen, as my body changed and my brain matured, I decided I could no longer take the oppression I felt living in that household. I decided to stand up to my father. What did I have to lose? Life really couldn't be any worse than it already was. I didn't feel loved in any way; nor did I feel like anyone cared about who I was as an individual. No one cared what I thought, including my opinions about God, sin, and a shift toward spirituality—which all very much departed from my upbringing.

My gut somersaulted at the thought of standing up for myself; it was a feeling so deep inside me, it was scary. But it told me I was doing the right thing, like maybe what I thought and felt had value. I did not know at the time that this "gut feeling" was instinct, that it was energy, *my* energy compelling me to further harness it and not let my father take it away yet again. That was my mindset on that crucial day when my father came home and I decided to confront him.

I remember my heart pounding out of my chest, but I harnessed that exhilarating and frightening feeling in my body, pointing me in the direction toward freedom. So at fourteen I used my energy for the first time to get me closer to what I needed, which was out of that house. Fear and excitement. This is the combined sensation of making a positive move. Allowing myself to feel the fear but not be deterred by it became a theme in my life; fear has an energy in and of itself. It creates a feeling of excitement and anticipation that *something* is going to change, most often for the better.

Thankfully I had rehearsed the exact words I was going to say—the words that would forever change the trajectory of my life. I closed my eyes and blurted, "Dad, I've never felt like I've been able to tell you how I feel, but I don't want to be here anymore."

"What do you mean you don't want to be here anymore?" he asked, completely surprised, yet devoid of emotion. "Where would you go?"

"I'll go live with Mom." Even though I heard from her only once or twice a year, I had hoped that moving in with my mother would be an option. I figured anything would be better than the circumstances I had been living in. To me, this man was not a father; I didn't feel any love from him or for him, only fear.

Dad stood up with his arms crossed and asked, "If I don't let you go, will you run away?" I hadn't thought that far ahead but answered yes, and that felt right too. In the back of my mind, I hoped he'd fight for me, that my threat would show him the error of his ways. And you know what he said?

"Okay, if that's what you want." Completely devoid of any emotions.

My father asked if I'd be willing to speak to our pastor about my feelings and my desire to go live with my mother even though I had been estranged from her for most of my childhood.

"You have a demon," the pastor said, "just like your mother." This judgment felt like a betrayal from a supposed holy man. All I could do was let the betrayal seep into my bones. Even a man of God didn't believe in me, didn't see my value, didn't help me out of a troubled circumstance. He just gave my father more reason to dig in his heels and see me as a threat to his control.

I left my father's house in Florida, saying goodbye to my four half-siblings, and moved across the country to California to be with my mother. Naturally it was scary to be jumping in to the complete unknown, but I rationalized that the unknown was better than the terrible known of my father's home. Moving in with her was a desperate measure, but I was living in a desperate time.

So I moved in with my mother and became a California girl and lived happily ever after.

Yeah, right.

Facing the Darkness

My struggle had just begun. I went from living in an incredibly strict home to living in one that was the opposite. No curfews, no check-ins, no mother-daughter meals, or bedtime rituals. Just a freshman in high school, I came and went as I pleased, no questions or concerns about academics, extracurricular activities, dating, or friends. I felt like I was not a daughter but a mere roommate. Since my mother lived in a one-bedroom apartment, I slept on the couch in the living room. Being that I was a rather sensitive child, the stress of all the change, being yet again the new kid on the block, and the lack of love being shown to me, I cried myself to sleep most nights.

When I was barely sixteen, I moved in with a neighbor and her nineteen-year-old daughter, who felt sorry for me and wanted to help me. By the time I moved out of my mother's house, I was completely emotionally numb. I dated boys who were way too old for me; I didn't see the value in my body, and I began to self-injure. I didn't feel anything. Not happy, not sad, not mad, not anything. I began skipping school until I stopped going. I didn't stay long with the neighbor because I didn't feel loved in that household either. Instead, I began bouncing around from my neighbors' to friends' houses and eventually to my grandparents' place. It was during this time that I had started thinking that I didn't want to live anymore, and I even made a few suicide attempts.

My first attempt was when I was seventeen. I felt like a zombie. Totally numb. I had no sense of grounding, no feeling of being loved or cared about by anyone but one set of grandparents, and no goals, hopes, or dreams. All I wanted was to die, to not exist. I kept these feel-ings to myself as I started plotting how I could kill myself. Given that I hated the feeling of physical pain, I wanted to find the least painful way to off myself.

After getting my GED, I started attending a local community college that my grandmother signed me up and paid for. While I was there, I befriended a guy who liked doing drugs of most any kind. I'd heard of peo-ple overdosing on drugs, so I thought maybe I could just OD on cocaine, or at least numb myself up enough to be able to cut an artery without feeling it. Through my friend, I got the phone number of a drug dealer.

Oddly, I was really excited that my plan was starting to come together. Excited to think of my death—at least it was some type of positive change to look forward to.

One day, after I'd saved up enough money, I called the drug dealer and asked to buy an 8 ball. I also bought some razor blades so I could carry out my plan. Still in my work uniform, I drove over to the drug dealer's place, picked up the cocaine, and then drove to the beach, park-ing in a condo building parking lot. I started doing the coke, though I really had no clue what I was doing. I got quite high pretty quickly but still had a lot more to do if I was going to try to OD.

What I didn't realize was that the parking lot had good security, and it was being patrolled by police. Someone at the condo must have reported an unrecognized car in the parking lot with someone inside. When a police officer shone his lights on me, I scurried into action. I tried hiding some of the cocaine that I had placed on my center console. But this didn't work out so well, and the white powder went all over the car. However, I was still determined to die that night. So before the offi-cer could ask me to step out of the car, I slipped one of the razor blades under the elastic band of my pants.

I was placed in the back of the police car while the officer and his partner searched my car. I was very high at that moment, but I thought to myself, *Now is the perfect time to slit my wrists.* I could easily die before they finished their search. So I pulled out the razor blade and cut my wrists, careful not to catch their attention. I delighted in the sight of the blood pooling up on the floorboard. I thought to myself, *I did it. I pulled it off.*

But it didn't take long for the cops to discover the drugs, finding enough that they decided to take me into custody. The original officer came over to the car to get me out of the back to handcuff me. I'll never forget the look on his face. I remember the horror, sadness, and bewilderment in his eyes when he realized what I had done. All I felt was proud of myself. I hoped there was still time for me to bleed to death before help could arrive.

I must have passed out because I don't remember the ambulance coming. I don't remember the hospital stay either. I do, however, remember being in a psychiatric ward for a week or two. During that time, I followed the rules and went with the program so they would think that I was going to pull through and be okay.

That wasn't the last time I attempted to kill myself. After each unsuccessful suicide attempt, I can vividly remember thinking that as soon as people were off my back and I no longer seemed like a suicide risk, I would be able to plot how to successfully kill myself the next time. I was hell-bent on dying, and so I pretended to be okay so I could fly under the radar, win my freedom back, and just die like I wanted to. In what turned out to be my final suicide attempt, I swallowed an entire bottle of antidepressants. This time I would have succeeded in my death wish had my boyfriend not found me convulsing and called an ambulance. At the hospital, my stomach was pumped, and I remained in a coma for many days.

Thankfully, I didn't die, and my grandparents were there to help me get back on my feet.

Trying for Stability

Many months after my recovery, when I was eighteen, I moved in with a friend and began working full time. During that time, I met a Dutch student on an exchange program at the local university and quickly fell in puppy love. After his semester was over, he returned to the Netherlands. We stayed in touch and talked of eventually being together and traveling the world. Soon after he left, I discovered I was pregnant. Neither one of us hesitated to say that we should have the baby and get married. He flew back to Florida and my grandparents threw us a quick little wedding, and off to Holland I moved. Getting pregnant with my son probably saved my life. As I mentioned, I was completely numb emotionally at that point in my life and had no stability. Knowing that I was responsible for someone outside myself and promising I would give him the emotional support and love that I never received, I found a calm and purpose like I had never experienced. The hormones from the pregnancy helped me start to feel emotions again. My new baby, young husband, and his family grounded me.

But our marriage quickly showed signs that we were incompatible. From my point of view, he treated me pretty terribly and put me down a lot. Being in a foreign country, living with his family, and not being able to provide for myself in a way that would allow me more independence made me feel even more powerless.

My low energy, lack of focus, and inner instinct that our marriage would not last made me turn inward in a search for answers and direction. I felt what had become a familiar energy surge in my gut, teaching me that my mood and energy level was a communication method to my soul, and it was to be trusted and heeded. I wasn't happy; I needed more, as something wasn't right. That funny feeling was there again, just as it had been when I was with my father and when I left my mother, showing me the right way—and that way was out. I made my needs known to my husband, stood my ground, and we moved back to the States, settling in Los Angeles.

With my son keeping me grounded with the love I had for him and the responsibility that came with being a parent, I became aware of my internal energy and started to pay attention to how I felt, how my energy felt in my body. My moods, emotions, and energy level became my compass. I began to notice when things felt good in my body and when they felt bad in my body. It was as if all those years of being emotionally numbed had taken a 180-degree turn, and I was opened up to feel all types of energy, good and bad, around me or within me. Listening to this instinct became natural, as I had no other outside confidants to guide me or help me process my circumstances.

After three years of living with my husband, I realized our marriage of obligation and convenience wasn't what I wanted for my life. I deserved more, as did my son. I deserved to be happy and enjoy life.

Telling my husband we would divorce wasn't the first time I had found the courage to walk away from the known and into the unknown, but this time I wasn't afraid. I trusted in my body's physical responses to his put-downs and negativity. I'd been there before—not valued—so in a way I knew how to move away from it, trusting in my experiences.

Nothing had killed me before, not attempts at dying at my own hand, not even a coma. I needed to love myself more than my husband and his needs. For a long time, I didn't even know what love was, let alone self-love. Anytime I owned my value and attempted self-love, I was told, "See ya!" This decision to love myself more than another person was a gift and would become my superpower.

Having the Courage to Self-Love

If you are living in a situation where you are not practicing self-love, it takes a lot of courage to take the first steps forward. It's scary to confront people you are in a relationship with, no matter what kind of relationship. It's a lot easier to play it safe, to be nice, and accept what someone is willing to give you. When I was in my teens and early twenties, it was easy to think to myself, *Sure, why not a few more years of harsh punishment or of being put down? Why not commit my life to living in a foreign country in which I feel stunted and alone? And what's a decade of toxic friendships and bad bosses and not having the confidence to go back to school?*

When you are giving all of your heart to someone or something outside of yourself, you are just running from the truth: You have handed your power to someone else and are now basing your value on other people's actions and beliefs.

Loving yourself more—acknowledging to yourself that you are worth more than what you are getting from others—is risky business, even riskier than staying in abusive, toxic situations. There are risks of losing relationships, sometimes even relationships you've invested a lot of time and energy into. And there is the immense emotional pain, confusion, and loss that comes with detaching from someone or something you've invested so much of yourself in.

But, in my experience, it's always been a risk worth taking; putting myself and my needs first has always paid off in spades. My commitment to loving myself more than anyone else, even someone I was willing to share my life with, goes well beyond romantic relationships. Choosing to love myself more means I don't allow anyone to treat me as if I have no value or to take from me the one thing I do have: power over myself.

When a friend has been toxic, self-centered, or harshly judgmental toward me, I've chosen to love myself more and say goodbye, with gratitude and grace. And when I've closed the door to these toxic relationships, I've immediately attracted much better relationships that would never have come my way had I not closed the door to the toxic ones.

> Choosing to love myself more means I don't allow anyone to treat me as if I have no value.

If a boss passed me over for a well-deserved promotion or a raise, I chose to love myself more and stand up for myself with dignity and respect. Anytime I've stood up for myself, I've upped my pay level and leveled up in my career.

If a family member took me for granted, played the blame game, or hurt me with words or otherwise, I chose to love me more, trusting that blood does not indebt us to one another. The result has always been less negativity in my life, less stress, less burden, and more joy and peace.

Finding Your Own Turning Point

As in every hero's journey, there comes a turning point, a pinnacle of understanding and a coming together, and my path was no different. At the divergent point where I chose myself above all others, I developed a deeper understanding of what it means to be human, of how hurt and loss operate, why badness exists, and how to use all of it to help me grow and love.

Self-love is knowing your value and standing up for your value, even if that means taking the risk of losing something in the external world. Any loss will be a temporary one. But the inner fire that gets stoked from standing up for your value just increases your value in the external world. It's looking internally instead of externally for the deep love we desire. True love first begins with yourself. Only when you truly love yourself can you attract like in kind.

Throughout the rest of this book, I share stories and wisdom from some of my favorite authors, psychologists, and trauma experts that helped me become the resilient person I am today, having overcome trauma, disappointment, and settling for less. Some chapters offer suggestions and ideas on how to move closer to self-love and how to recognize when that love is vulnerable, while other chapters address what to do when you find yourself slipping, feeling "less than" or "not worth it," and allowing others to steal your energy and your power.

I do all of this purely anecdotally, as I believe that stories—relatable, honest, vulnerable stories—are what truly connect and help people. And besides, I have nothing more to offer you than my own experiences. No doubt about it, I am no expert. I'm not a guru with pages of published research, not a credentialed anybody with a pocketful of PhDs. I am an expert in me, only me, specializing in *my* circumstances and beliefs that planted the seeds of self-loathing. I am the expert only on what I practiced and still do to harness the energy within me and wrestle with it, juggle it, and manipulate it until it represents and embodies who I know I was meant to be in this world.

When I think back to my younger years, I only wish that I learned how to love myself much earlier on in my life. I'm so grateful that I did eventually learn how important it was to adopt a conscious self-love practice. I'm hoping that my experiences will help you come to that same understanding for yourself.

Chapter 2

The Truth and Hope
of an Elusive Emotion

You're already stuck with yourself for a lifetime. Why not
improve this relationship?
—Veronika Tugaleva, *The Art of Talking to Yourself*

For much of my life, I found the easier choice was to live without self-love, to act in the best interests of others rather than myself. But, ironically, in doing so, I made my own life more difficult.

We know what it looks like when people don't love themselves; the news is rife with stories and examples. Closer to home, we know people—or we *are* people—who do not practice self-love. Such people hide out in relationships that don't serve them, stay in crap jobs because they don't want to rattle the cages of their bosses; they overeat or undereat or drink too much or pull away from people who want to love them. They say "can't" and "won't" too much, stare too harshly in the mirror with criticism, and don't connect with nature, themselves, or their God. They don't recognize their innate talents or gifts, and if they do, they squander them. They compare themselves to others, thinking success and happiness are for the masses and not for them, and rely on outside situations or people to validate their existence and value. They get sick, physically and mentally, rely too heavily on medications, and do not take care of their medical needs. They are angry, hostile, jealous, depressed, and anxious. Or they overextend, overachieve, overcompensate, overpromise, and overdeliver. They do all the "overs" in an attempt to prove their worth to the outside world.

If you have ever done any of the following, you are giving your power away, and therefore not practicing self-love:

- Constantly sacrificing your time, energy, and talents to others, expecting them to give back what you give: at home, at work, and with friends, family, and others
- Feeling resentful, hurt, and even angry at people who don't treat you the way you treat them
- Putting off your own interests or hobbies because you worry that pursuing them will take away from time needed for others in your life, like your friends, boyfriend, children, bosses, and so on
- Feeling shame about something about yourself; not letting go of mistakes, regrets for things you didn't do, or things said, or lapses in judgment that happened in the past
- Not taking care of your health, fitness, or hygiene
- Staying in unhealthy relationships
- Not valuing yourself at work by not asking for a raise or promotion or a new, challenging project
- Not setting boundaries or allowing someone to cross boundaries because of being scared to speak up for yourself or out of fear of making someone else feel bad
- Not saying no to others when that's what you feel like saying
- Letting friends or family put you down or make you feel "less than"

Do you recognize yourself in any of these examples? It's not an *exhaustive* list of the ways we give away our power, but it is an *exhausting* list. All that power, all that energy given away in all circumstances, in all types of relationships, all hours of the day. Regaining that energy is one benefit you'll see from pursuing the truth and hope of self-love.

Three Components of Self-Love

The dictionary defines self-love as "regard for one's own well-being and happiness."[1] There are three types of self-love:

- Physical—how you view your physical self
- Mental—how you think of yourself (self-acceptance)
- Psychological—how you treat yourself (self-respect)

I look back on so many instances in my life where my lack of self-love manifested in one or all three of these areas. When I moved away from my father's strict and abusive upbringing and into my mother's neglectful and mentally abusive home, I was searching for ways to fill the void in my heart with love. I searched outward, looking to others to fill the gaps in my life, with very little regard for the sanctity of my body. Giving away myself far too young and too often to boys older than me, I viewed my physical self not as something to be valued and respected but as a catalyst to get to what I thought I needed: an act of love, albeit superficial and short-lived.

Jeffrey Borenstein, MD, president and CEO of the Brain & Behavior Research Foundation, puts his pragmatic lens on self-love, taking it out of the "nice to have" box and positioning it where it needs to be: as basic human *necessity*. Dr. Borenstein says, "Self-love is a state of appreciation for oneself that grows from actions that support our physical, psychological, and spiritual growth. Self-love means having a high regard for your own well-being and happiness. Self-love means taking care of your own needs and not sacrificing your well-being to please others. Self-love means not settling for less than you deserve."[2]

Self-love can mean something different for each person because we all have many different lenses on life, unique experiences and biases, and various ways to take care of ourselves. But one thing is for certain: We need to support our growth through our own actions, not the actions of others. Determining what self-love looks like for you as an individual is what Dr. Borenstein says is "an important part of your mental health."[3] This book is dedicated to supporting you in your pursuit to figuring out what self-love is to you and how to apply it in your life so you can support your growth and healing.

Taking Responsibility for Your Happiness

Elyse Santilli, an award-nominated life coach, manifestation teacher, and the host of the *Wake Up and Manifest* podcast, says, "Self-care is not selfish; it is essential. When you get so busy with to-do lists and work and giving to others that you forget to make time for self-care and pleasure, your cup is going to run dry and then you have nothing left for anyone."[4] Elyse teaches that when we focus on doing what makes us feel good, we show up for our family and friends full of loving energy and have more love to give to them. We realize that no one can make us as happy as we can make ourselves, and that no one else, no matter how close they are to us, is responsible for our happiness. You have probably heard about the resentment people have toward those who are close to them, and many times that resentment can be avoided by not relying on them for our happiness. Our happiness will come authentically from within.

I remember once sitting in my car in a parking lot at a Whole Foods store just incessantly thinking negatively about my boyfriend at the time and how I felt he had undervalued and neglected me. Then there was a moment that I became conscious of this thinking pattern and thought, *Why am I letting these negative feelings have such a grip on me? What is it that I need right now that I'm not getting from him?* I decided at that moment that I was going to flip the way I was thinking about things.

So I went into Whole Foods and bought some aromatherapy items and something yummy I could eat at home. I decided I would take a hot bubble bath and pamper myself—to give myself the love and attention I had been seeking from my boyfriend. I also decided I wasn't going to think about him at all. Rather, I was going to focus my attention on making myself relaxed and happy. When I carried out my plan, I felt instantly good. My energy completely shifted from negative to positive. When my boyfriend came home, he just wanted to put his arms around me because I was emanating such positive energy. Funny thing, I got what I had been wanting from him because I chose to give it to myself. I realized at that moment that it's really only me who should be responsible for my happiness, not anyone else. It's unfair to put that burden on anyone else. And no one else could ever really make me as happy as I could make myself when I needed it.

Self-Love Is Unconditional

We crave unconditional love from those close to us. But the truth is, love is and should be conditional from others. Other people need to have their own boundaries in place for what they will and will not tolerate from others, regardless of their relationship with you. It is only self-love that can truly be unconditional. If you make it your priority to give unconditional love to yourself first and foremost, above anyone else, there will never be a reason to feel like you need to chase that feeling outside of yourself.

I like to think of self-love as you being your lover, mother, father, and so on, so that you bestow on yourself what we've been conditioned to think only someone else can and should give us. Why wait for that boyfriend to come along to show you the love you've been waiting for or treat you to a vacation, jewelry, or a nice dinner?

Don't do what I did, which was put all my eggs in the basket of romantic love. Somehow, for much of my life, I'd been searching for an elusive, deep connection with someone that I always thought would give me the feeling of deep love. Mistakenly, I thought that it could only be found in romantic relationships. And so pursuing relationships, looking for my soul mate, was always a deeply embedded mission of mine.

When I first moved in with my boyfriend Dave (mentioned in the introduction), whom I deeply loved and believed would be my life partner, I gave myself to him. Almost immediately after I began doing housework for him and helping him with his business and his psychological needs, he began to pull away. I felt disconnected and nothing like a life partner at all. I could've been just another one of his friends or family members that he relied on for constant help! I wasn't feeling valued, and he made it clear that I was not his priority. With him, I was not expanding and growing as an individual. I felt stagnant.

As I came to understand, thinking that my romantic relationship determined my value as a person was the opposite of self-love. Had I only put more of that energy into fostering my love for myself over the years, the love I sought would have already been there, before any new relationship began. I've come to understand that all relationships are a reflection of your relationship with yourself. If you are not deeply in love with yourself, no one else will be either.

When you practice self-love, *you put your energy back into your soul and grow your self-power*. Thankfully my trusty instinct helped me get out of a situation that was unhealthy. I notice now that exuding my powerful energy attracts people who want to know me, who say I'm beautiful when I have my hair in a ratty bun and sheet marks on my cheek. They want to go into business with me, believing me to be creative and competent. They trust me and my power, because my energy exudes self-love and confidence. We will talk about the synergistic relationship of self-love, power, and energy in a later chapter.

When you love yourself and accept your humanity and inevitable flaws, it helps you work past insecurities, makes you less needy, and helps you get out of toxic relationships. When you retain your power, you change your energy and people become drawn to you. Suddenly your partner will treat you better as a result of you treating yourself better.

Finding love from within will mean far more to you in the long run, as it builds up your personal power; and when you have personal power, you are happier, more fulfilled, more focused, and give more to those you love. Relying on or expecting someone else to give you value means you give up your self-worth and power to others. If that external person no longer bestows what you want, or ceases to be in your life, so goes your sense of being worthy.

Self-Love Is Not Selfish or Narcissistic

It is important to understand the difference between selfishness and self-love. It's the confusion between the two that leads many of us to forgo self-love because we've been conditioned to think it is selfish.

Women, in particular, come into the world with much power. Our energy supports entire families. But we have been conditioned to give that power away to others. *We have been incorrectly told that putting ourselves first is selfish, and so we feel guilty if we aren't naturally giving our energy away to others.* And then the children leave, or the marriage breaks up, and there we are, alone, unequipped to pick up the bricks and build a house of self-love for ourselves.

This cycle can be stopped when our power always resides within. We have to shift things and keep some of that love for ourselves. We don't have to give all our love away to others. In fact, the more we keep our love burning within, the more love we have to give to the world.

But it is exactly this fear and guilt that keep us from loving ourselves. Who conditioned us to think and behave this way? Who knows? But its pervasiveness is evident in every culture around the world.

After years of working with hundreds of patients, psychologist Vanessa Scotto has found that not knowing the difference between selfishness and self-love is one of the biggest causes of exhaustion, anxiety, and unhappiness. She says that many of us are grappling with what she calls the "fear of selfishness syndrome." *The fear of being selfish causes us to believe that we should be doing whatever it takes to support others, even if it is to our own personal detriment, or diminishes our vital energy.*

"Only when you act out of fear of being selfish you wear yourself thin," Scotto says. "Ultimately you begin to feel overwhelmed, overloaded, and perhaps even resentful. Worn out and trapped by your own guilt mechanism, you lose the ability to show up for others with joyful generosity."[5]

To be selfish is to lack consideration or concern for others, to be concerned only with yourself regardless of others, or at the expense of others. Self-love, on the other hand, is putting your own needs first. It is not at the *expense* of others. You can still have consideration for others while putting your own needs above anyone else's. Who else is going to care for you and meet your own needs as much as you can?

As you get ready to take your own self-love journey, be prepared that people may accuse you of being selfish. My mother did just that. And if she had had more power or influence in my life, her words might have actually hindered my self-love journey more than they did. If someone calls you selfish, it's your job to decide whether you are being selfish or if you are just giving yourself the love you need. If you are doing something that makes you feel good, then *you* are doing the right thing for *you*. Remember: Your intuition would tell you otherwise. If you're on the ceiling, then fantastic. So what if other people are looking up at you from the floor! Beware of naysayers who try to convince you not to make the right decision for you, even when that decision makes you feel good. I discuss naysayers more in Part II.

In the same way that self-love is not selfish, it is not narcissistic either. Narcissism is the opposite of self-love. Narcissists have an inflated version of their

> If you are doing something that makes you feel good, then *you* are doing the right thing for *you*.

sense of importance. They need an excessive amount of attention and admiration from others and have a sense of entitlement. Narcissism is in fact a personality disorder. Narcissists can be manipulative, demeaning, and lack empathy. They can be preoccupied with external factors such as beauty, power, and success. I was raised by narcissists, and they taught me to not love myself.

It's very important to make the distinction between self-love and narcissism, because as women, we tend to be so afraid of coming off as selfish or narcissistic—so much so that we run away from anything that we think might be perceived as such. Self-compassion expert Kristin Neff, an associate professor of human development at the University of Texas at Austin, has found that the biggest reason people aren't more self-compassionate is that they are afraid they'll become self-indulgent. Dr. Neff says, "They believe self-criticism is what keeps them in line. Most people have gotten it wrong because our culture says being hard on yourself is the way to be."[6]

Self-love is about putting yourself and your needs as your first priority and not expecting anyone else to do it for you. In fact, if you rely on someone else to put your needs first for you, you are essentially giving your power away to someone else, which is not self-love. I did this far too many times, especially in romantic relationships, thinking my partner's actions toward me should be geared to my every happiness. This is far from reality and frankly unfair to both people in the relationship. In Part II, I reveal many other things—aside from making it the responsibility of others to love you—that prevent us from practicing self-love.

Self-Love Is Power

Just as there are many words to describe the ways people do not love themselves—self-judgment, diminishment, self-criticism, self-abandonment, devaluing—there are words that represent ways we self-love:

Self-compassion, self-care, and self-forgiveness are three of the most popular synonyms.

But, in my experience, nothing represents self-love more than *power*. Your love is your power. To love yourself, you must know, own, and retain your power. You must believe it rests in you and that you are one with it.

When you do not love yourself, you do not possess your power or control; when you do not own your power or control, you are not loving yourself. Self-love and power are interdependent.

Self-Love Will Help Your Career

Even business-minded *Forbes* magazine has reported on the benefits of self-love on careers and in business. When you practice self-love, you do not operate out of fear any longer. Therefore, you take more risks, decrease the inner critic's voice, care less about what other people think, and experience less burnout. You have the confidence to apply for jobs that you might have disqualified yourself from. And you have the power to stand up for yourself and require to be compensated based on your own sense of self-value. Self-love in career success and in entrepreneurship is so important and transformative, I have dedicated an entire chapter to it (see Chapter 17).

Chapter 3

Self-Love Is Life's Vitamin

Today you are you! That is truer than true!
There is no one alive who is you-er than you!
Shout loud, "I am lucky to be what I am!"
—Dr. Seuss, *Happy Birthday to You!*

Giving away ourselves and swallowing our own needs makes us sick, tired, anxious, and depressed. In contrast, regularly practicing self-love is like taking a vitamin that brings energy and joy into your life. If you don't believe me, let's look at the research.

The Science of Self-Love

In empirically driven fields, research is being conducted on the practice of self-love. From neuroscience to psychology to exercise physiology, people want to know how the practice of self-love heals, fulfills, and drives us closer to ourselves and our potential. The evidence of the power of self-love in the health of our bodies, minds, and souls is hard to deny.

Dr. Kristin Neff has conducted extensive research and written books on the subject. The research suggests that taking a break from being hard on ourselves and accepting our flaws may be a starting point toward better health. Of Neff's research, the *New York Times* reported, "People who score high on tests of self-compassion have less depression and anxiety and tend to be happier and more optimistic. Preliminary data suggest that self-compassion can even influence how much we eat and may help some people lose weight."[1]

Taking part in compassion exercises has been found to calm the heart rate and switch off the body's fight-or-flight response. Other studies have shown that this threat response damages the immune system. Researchers believe the ability to switch off this response may lower the risk of disease. What this suggests is that when we are in a constant state of anxiety because we are beating ourselves up or not supporting our needs, we are opening ourselves up for disease. In a study published in the journal *Clinical Psychological Science*, 135 healthy University of Exeter students were divided into five groups, and members of each group listened to a different set of audio instructions. The two groups who received instructions to be kind to themselves said they felt more self-compassion and connection with others and showed a bodily response reflecting feelings of relaxation and safety. Their heart rates dropped and showed variation in length of time between heartbeats—a healthy sign of a heart that can respond flexibly to circumstances. They also showed lower sweat response.

On the other hand, recorded instructions that incited an inner voice of criticism led to an increased heart rate and a higher sweat response—consistent with emotions of threat and distress. Dr. Hans Kirschner, who conducted the research as the study's first author at Exeter, said, "These findings suggest that being kind to oneself switches off the threat response and puts the body in a state of safety and relaxation that is important for regeneration and healing."[2]

Lead researcher Dr. Anke Karl, of the University of Exeter, said in an online interview, "Self-compassion [is] related to higher levels of wellbeing and better mental health. . . . Our study is helping us understand the mechanism of how being kind to yourself when things go wrong could be beneficial in psychological treatments. By switching off our threat response, we boost our immune systems."[3]

The American Psychological Association agrees that self-compassion correlates with better physical and mental health. In people with diabetes, studies show stabilized glucose levels. In other participants, self-compassion increased immune function and relaxation. Studies have also associated lower levels of self-compassion with mental health concerns like anxiety, depression, and posttraumatic stress disorder.[4]

Self-compassion has also been a treatment in eating disorders, disordered eating, and body image issues. It is not surprising that most individuals with eating disorders also lack self-compassion. Being overly critical of oneself is often at the base of behaviors of those with different types of eating disorders; in many recovery programs, self-compassion is introduced as its antidote.

In a blog post for the Eating Recovery Center, Joanna Nolan wrote about self-compassion and its power in her recovery journey: "Having compassion for yourself doesn't mean you have to love yourself every moment of every day—but that you honor your humanness. . . . The more we open ourselves and our hearts to the reality of this . . . the more we are able to feel compassion for ourselves."[5]

I couldn't agree more with the previous statement. In fact, I'd go a bit further and say that practicing self-love doesn't always feel good at the onset. Practicing self-love sometimes requires painful decisions, breaking up with people you love, standing up to an authority figure, facing a fear, defending your boundaries, or telling somebody no when you are used to people pleasing. Sometimes I have to go through emotional pain and heartache for a bit to make the right decisions for myself, but it's always worth it to fight for myself through the pain. In the end, the risk, the discomfort, and the fear help me emerge feeling more alive.

Becoming Connected to the Universe

I've come to learn that self-love is our connection to the universe. Since as far back as I can remember, I've always had a fundamental feeling that we are part of God, that we are not separate from God. Although I couldn't quite put my finger on what the meaning of God was to me as a youth.

Given my extremely religious upbringing, now that I reflect back on how I felt about being one with God, it really was a visionary perspective at the time, as I had no external input giving me this kind of perspective in my youth. My nature is to observe and come to my own beliefs about things, and I hope to inspire you to do the same. What I saw in the church as a youth is that this third party worked very hard to make people believe that the church and belief in the concepts of the modern Bible were our *only* connection to God—that anything else, any other religion or practice or thought, was evil. But despite the daily programming by my parents, to me, you didn't need the church or the Bible to connect to a higher power. And you didn't have to put a religious label on faith.

I would think, *Why are we giving our power away? This would never happen if we realized our own power, not letting anyone else take it from us, realizing that a truly loving God would have never created us only to have us treat ourselves and others so terribly as religions make us believe we should.*

Of course, when I dared to state my point of view to my parents (when I got old enough to dare to have my own opinion), I was labeled "evil" by my family and our church. The pastor said I had inherited a demon from my mother. This was all shortly before I left home at the age of fourteen to go live with my mother. I lived as an atheist until I was twenty-four.

While my life's journey has naturally led me on a path toward deepening my love of myself and my relationship with myself, I only recently have come to understand the importance of self-love not only as a spiritual practice but also as a gift and a duty to receive.

I recently read Anita Moorjani's book, *Dying to Be Me*. I'd heard of Anita Moorjani many years ago through the work of Dr. Wayne Dyer. In her book, Moorjani shares her experience on her deathbed in the hospital, how her organs shut down from terminal cancer, and how she died and crossed over.

Through the death of her physical body and transport to the spirit world, Moorjani says she realized how magnificent we are, that she had caused her own cancer and that she had the power to heal herself. She was given the choice to come back to the physical world or to cross over. She chose to come back into her body with her new understanding of life. She realized she could heal herself. And she actually did heal herself, miraculously, in just weeks. All the cancer that had plagued her for years was gone.

She writes, "My body created the cancer because of all my dumb thoughts, judgments about myself, limiting beliefs, all of which caused me so much internal turmoil. If only I'd known that we are supposed to come here and feel good about ourselves and about life and just express ourselves and have fun with it."[6]

She says her experience showed her that the best way to connect to the universal life force energy is from within. It starts with loving and trusting yourself. The more you are able to do so, the more centered you feel in the cosmic tapestry. The more connected each of us feels individually, the more we are able to touch others, enabling others to feel the same.

Self-love is our way back to divinity, our true self. How can we realize our own magnificence if we don't like ourselves or treat ourselves well, let alone love ourselves? Well, my goal is to help eliminate this question from your life. From here on, you are on the path to your potential and inner peace. We now know what self-love is and what it isn't. We know it is connected to our power and our energy and that they work synergistically with the universe. We know we need it to live and to thrive and to be healthy. It is a gift and our duty to receive, and it is the way to a life of well-being and connectedness.

In the next part of the book, I talk about recognizing the saboteurs of self-love—the things that we do or allow others to do—that prevent us from the practice and threaten our universally bestowed gift. Only then can we be open and prepared to receive our own love.

A Holistic Effect

There is a plethora of studies that show mental self-love is necessary to well-being, but what about the physical and psychological aspects of self-love? It turns out that putting yourself first improves your romantic relationships and boosts your career success. It connects you with spiritual sources and guides you to a better sense of your needs.

For me, consciously choosing to put myself first connected me even more in my spiritual practice. As discussed, it got me closer to God than I had ever been before. So many religions and dogmas of the past taught us to deny our bodies. Now I truly understand for myself what Eckhart Tolle means when he says, "Transformation is through the body, not away from it."[7] Our inner body is our connection to the universe, bringing us closer to our understanding that we are all connected as one.

Chapter 4

Tuning In to Your
Energy and Power

have always been in tune with how much energy I have and whether it
is positive or negative. Even as a young adult, when I felt low or unmotivated, sad or disheartened, insecure, guilty, shameful—you name it—I
knew these feelings were much more than emotional reactions. They
were messages. Low-energy Jenna signaled something was not right
and that I was not acting in my own best interests. I didn't quite know
it then, but my low-energy response told me I was not loving myself or
treating myself in the ways a person does when she shows herself love.
Low energy fueled even lower energy, and, as discussed in Chapter 3,
the fear-and-flight response was ignited, putting me in a constant state of
depression, confusion, and self-loathing. Throughout this book I share
several stories of how these energy messages helped me take action and
make change, even in the face of the most difficult circumstances.

It is my experience that when trying to develop self-love and make it
a lifelong practice, you must be in touch with energy—your energy, the
energy of others—and listen to what it is telling you. Energy is a guide
toward or away from self-love. This begs to be emphasized. *Energy is a
guide toward or away from self-love*. If you aren't in touch with what your
energy feels like, you will always be giving it away, because you don't
know the value of what you possess.

When you always nurture your energy within your body, you empower yourself. Once you get used to the amazing feeling of energy flowing through you, propelling you and hugging you, when it's gone, you notice. When I would start to feel depleted or not able to feel my energy, I wouldn't recognize myself.

The Danger of Being Comfortably Numb

At one point in my life, I lived with a boyfriend named Jerry (more on him later in the book). I remember quite vividly feeling like I couldn't feel my energy; it was as though the electric charge I once had for life went dull. I missed that beautiful feeling I used to have in my body. I guess I was comfortably numb.

At that time, I hadn't yet placed a high enough value on myself and my energy to leave the situation. Not that it was a bad situation for most of our time together. But we weren't energetically matched either. Perhaps I was unconsciously trading my energy for what he provided me: stability, family, love. I came to find out later that he put on a mask, covering who he really was, to keep me around. But the low-energy vibes should have been my clue that I wasn't living authentically or in my best interest. I came to see who he really was when he took off his mask, and that's when I decided I needed to love me more, even if it meant disrupting both our lives.

I took some time away from him and carved out my own space for about two weeks. I needed to be by myself, spending time with friends and doing things that nurtured me and raised my vibrations. For that time, Jerry, at my request, agreed he wouldn't contact me so I could contemplate our relationship without his presence in my life.

In just that short time being away from him and temporarily cutting off the channel of communication, I felt my energy turn back on. Damn, how I had missed it. I woke up unburdened. I felt like I was alive again, wanted to be back in nature, feeling inspired and invigorated, full of hope and possibilities. That was a big sign for me that being on my own put me on the right path energetically. I needed to listen to my increased energy message and leave Jerry for good. When you love yourself, you do what the universe wants you to do. You raise your vibrations to match the higher frequencies of the universe. We meet up with Jerry again in Chapter 23 when we talk more about the importance of taking space and why doing so is an act of self-love and self-commitment.

Self-Love Provides Positive Energy

Self-love fills you with positive energy, just like a power chord energizes a phone, because loving yourself makes you more compassionate, tolerant, courageous, and authentic. Those acts lift you up. What is more, when you resonate with the universe's intentions, your vibrations go up many notches. Pat Longo, spiritual healer and author of *The Gifts of Your Anxiety: Simple Spiritual Tools to Find Peace, Awaken the Power Within, and Heal Your Life,* calls the ability to listen to and use your negative feelings "intuition." Human bodies are made up of electromagnetic energy, which means we vibrate at a certain frequency. We want to raise our vibration to operate on a higher, more powerful level. She writes, "When you're depressed, going through trauma, experiencing a loss, dealing with an addiction, or just feeling sad, your vibration is low, it's on the floor."[1] Longo connects elevating one's power and elevating one's energy as going hand-in-hand, using an example of a scene in the 1964 Disney movie *Mary Poppins.*

Pragmatic Mary Poppins and her friend Bert, along with the children Mary cares for, Jane and Michael, visit Uncle Albert. They are surprised to see Uncle Albert is sullen. Bert begins to tell a few jokes to lighten the mood, and they start to laugh. With each bout of laughter, Uncle Albert floats higher and higher in the room, until they are all on the ceiling, literally, singing the song "I Love to Laugh." Longo says,

"When we engage in something we love . . . we send our souls to the ceiling. We are operating on a high level, on what attracts only positivity and one that is closer to our authentic selves."[2]

We need our power and our energy to be firing on all circuits, and to do that, we need to engage in the exercises of self-love, the things that make us feel good and put us first on our priority list. I'm hoping this book will give you such tools, but for now here is a quick peek at some of the things Pat Longo suggests to keep your energy positive and your power boosted.

- Laugh
- Listen to music
- Meditate
- Practice gratitude
- Exercise
- Dance
- Prayer
- Faith and love[3]

As Gabby Bernstein says, "We're meant to feel good, that's the true nature of who we are. We think we need to chase that thing that will make us feel good, but the irony of it is that when we feel good, we'll get all of the things we want."[4]

If you want to be in a place where you are getting what you want in life, it's your responsibility to ensure you feel good throughout your day. I've personally committed to myself to make sure that I am not just satisfied with each day but in a state of feeling elated, exuberant, and fulfilled. I've found a simple way to help me do this. It's what I call my joy list. This list is personal to me and it's what makes me happy. It's just a simple list of things that I can do easily and instantly to put me in my happy place. My list includes listening to music, talking to or meeting up with a friend, going for a walk on a nice day, reading my favorite spiritual book, painting, playing tennis, looking at art from some of my favorite artists, and watching funny animal videos.

What Is Your Joy List?

Pull out your journal and make your own joy list of any quick and easy things you can do at any time to boost your spirit and charge up your power container. Side note: I also like to place my joy list on a sticky note that sits right by my computer. It reminds me to regularly do things that put me in my happy place.

Monitoring Your Power Container

Imagine you have a container that rests in your soul—your power container—and it's where your energy is stored. When my power container is full, I am nothing short of radiant. I blast my favorite music, plan get-togethers and BBQs with friends, feel invincible in attacking my goals, and am driven and ambitious, not to mention my house becomes super organized!

You can imagine what it feels like when that container empties, as it has been known to do. I don't want any music playing, I want to isolate, and I'm incredibly irritable. I'm drained and unmotivated, feel negative toward others, and am pessimistic about my future. My closet is a mess; dishes pile up in the sink.

I've found this concept of a power container to have very practical benefits in how I live my life. Every day, I try to monitor the level of energy in my power container and use that information to guide my decisions. If I'm in a situation where my energy feels low, I try to figure out why. Is my intuition telling me there's something wrong about the situation that I need to pay attention to? Have I not been practicing self-love, so I don't have any energy to share with others? And if my energy is high, then I know that I'm making good choices for myself.

Your love is your power. This is a motto that I've come to live by. I've often been told how "strong" I am by my friends, coworkers, and others who've witnessed the difficult moments in my life when I've chosen to put myself, my needs, and my happiness first. My love for myself is what gives me my strength. When we refuse to love and accept ourselves, we cut ourselves off from the energy that sustains life. This process happens gradually until we are disconnected from energy—the life force. And this leads to health issues, mental health problems, and the inability to live life to our fullest potential, among other things.

> Making peace with who you are—good and bad—is the deepest act of self-love and compassion.

Not loving yourself puts you in a battle with yourself. This is a fight you cannot win as this depletes your power, your vital energy. It's important to accept that we are flawed and make mistakes. But just as we accept our downsides, we must accept and applaud our strengths, and sometimes the only strength we might have in that moment is accepting our weaknesses. Making peace with your inner turmoil is critical to health and fulfillment. Making peace with who you are—good and bad—is the deepest act of self-love and compassion. Your energy and power can't help but increase, and your energy will attract like energy. This book and the chapters that remain will inspire you to fix your inner world, so you can reap the rewards and sanctity of the outer one.

How Do You Feel about Loving Yourself Unconditionally?

This is a good time to take a moment to reflect on your own feelings that you may have about the idea of loving yourself and putting yourself first. Write down in your journal anything that comes to mind. Don't overthink it or edit yourself. The key is just to let it flow. There is no right or wrong way to journal, and no one is going to read this but you. This is just a way to get to know your yourself better. Below are some journal prompts that may help you tune in to your current beliefs around self-love.

Write each prompt down in your journal, one at a time, filling in the blank space at the end of each sentence with your own words.

- If I put my own needs first in my life, above anyone else's needs, _____
- If I choose to do what really makes me happy, I feel like this will _____
- The ways in which I'm currently not putting myself first on my list include _____
- Currently, those who are the highest priority in my life, above myself, are _____
- I probably learned how to set those who are the highest priorities in my life from _____
- If I made myself my biggest priority in my life, the effect it would have on others would be _____
- If I practiced more self-love and self-compassion, the effect on my life would be _____

Once you can identify your own beliefs surrounding the concept of loving yourself first, as well as gaining an understanding as to where those beliefs might have come from, you can then better determine whether they are truly valid for you today. It then becomes easier to usher in new concepts around self-love and what would actually be best for you, based on what feels good to you.

PART II

How Do I Not Love Thee?
Seven Saboteurs of Self-Love

"How do I love thee? / Let me count the ways." The famous first lines of Sonnet 43, written by Elizabeth Barrett Browning in the mid-nineteenth century, are said to have been written for her husband, poet Robert Browning. When it comes to the expression of love for another person, the sentiments are universal. But in my life when it came to loving others first, I'd need more than ten fingers and toes to count the ways.

If only there were a poem that asked, "How do I love *me*? Let me count the ways," I might have been led to my self-awareness of these saboteurs sooner and not spent so many years feeding the outside sources that sabotaged my ability to self-love. I'm hoping you can learn from my experience.

I'm a bit of a self-help junkie and have done a ton of self-reflection, working on improving myself over the years. I am no stranger to the realities that trauma and attachment issues influenced my early childhood development. That's perhaps why, as an adult, I kept digging deeper into my situations and behavior patterns to understand my actions and responses so I can identify the things that have prevented me from practicing self-love.

When determining "How do I *not* love thee," I've experienced and counted the following seven ways.

1. Needing external validation or approval
2. Allowing social conditioning and programming to guide behavior
3. Letting guilt override you
4. Relying on false hope
5. Ignoring your intuition
6. Never saying no
7. Having self-limiting beliefs

Some of these factors are insidious, while others are so socially acceptable that it's hard to forget they're not good for us. The rest are pesky critters that are here to stay but are manageable with enough practice and awareness. And though I discuss them as separate factors, in reality you'll find that they are often interconnected (for example, social conditioning can lead to limiting beliefs, which leads us to ignore our intuition).

The key message I want you to take away is that it's just as important to recognize what keeps us from self-love as it is to understand the nature of self-love. Just like pilots who learn to fly with mastery must do so by simulating headwinds, bird strikes, and lightning, we must get up close and personal with the weather patterns that threaten our wellness and our goals to love ourselves more.

The need to identify which of these saboteurs are present in your own life is why I've included journaling suggestions in every chapter of this part of the book. They will help you think through situations you've faced and decisions you've made that are inconsistent with practicing self-love. I hope you will use the following chapters and journal prompts to help identify the threats in your life that may sabotage your journey to self-love.

Chapter 5

Needing External Validation or Approval

People are unhappy in large part because they are confused about what is valuable.
—William Irvine, *A Guide to the Good Life*

Sometimes after we make a decision or take action, we get caught in a trap of looking for approval from others to validate what we've done. To be fair, we are conditioned to live in this way. And even though I'm highly aware of the pitfalls of looking for external approval, I still find myself defaulting to this conditioning quite often. For most of us, it's our automatic mode. We can't help it; it's how we were brought up. For example, in social situations I often catch myself looking to others to see if they are accepting me or what I have to say, if I'm fitting in, if they think I'm attractive, or if they like me.

Positive reinforcement and extrinsic rewards for doing what's "right" or pleasing another person is a widespread practice. A child stops wetting the bed and receives stickers or candy. An adolescent girl loses her baby fat over the summer and is suddenly popular at school. A young executive works late nights, sacrifices a personal life, does the work of colleagues, and is promoted for hard work.

Of course, we want to know we are doing something right and that our hard work is noticed. But when reinforcement and rewards are misinterpreted as representations of love or worthiness, seeking such external validation interferes with or can even replace the act of loving ourselves. And that's when self-love sabotage begins. Let's look in more detail at how this happens.

What Are You Comparing Yourself To?

Deepak Chopra's book *The Seven Spiritual Laws of Success* is like my Bible; I've probably read it at least forty times. It helped turn the light bulb on for me when it came to my own need for validation. When we are influenced by ourselves and refer to our own spirit as a guide to who we are and how much we love ourselves, Chopra calls this *self-referral*—that is, we use our own internal beliefs and values as our point of reference. Chopra talks about how the opposite of self-referral is *object-referral*, which is when we are impacted by situations, circumstances, people, and things outside of ourselves. He writes, "In object-referral we are constantly seeking the approval of others. Our thinking and our behavior are always in anticipation of a response. It is therefore fear-based."[1]

If you find yourself relying on the approval of others and investing your self-worth in that approval, you are living on shaky ground. This is a fear-based way of living, and it breeds insecurity. If what you do feels good to you, then that's all you really need, regardless of what others think or choose to label you. Constantly posting selfies on Facebook or Instagram and then feeling good or bad based on the number of likes you get is not self-love. Even if you're getting a million likes, this shouldn't have anything to do with how you feel about yourself. If that is the case, then on a day when nobody gives you the thumbs-up, you will find yourself spiraling in unworthiness and more fear.

One of the insidious aspects of object-referral is how we let our egos, the false self, drive our sense of value. *I am good, I am worthy, because this guy likes me; the boss needs me; my parent is proud of me; I have this job title; I drive this car.*

We are not, however, our ego. That is why, in the end, no one ever ends up finding true happiness or success in these external sources. The ego is our social mask, the roles we play out in the world; the person we want everyone else to believe us to be. The perfect family on Facebook; the great accolades we boast on our websites; the celebrities who retweeted our posts. Our social masks thrive on approval. "Being ego-based power," writes Chopra, "it lasts only as long as the object of reference is there. If you have a certain title—if you're the president of the country or the chairman of a corporation—or if you have a lot of money, the power you enjoy goes with the title, with the job, with the money. Ego-based power will only last as long as those things last. As soon as the title, the job, the money go away, so does the power."[2]

Fear of rejection, fear of not fitting in, fear of not being liked or loved takes a lot out of a person. How can anyone really love you, or how can you really love yourself, when you live in such a precarious state of self?

Of course, we all want to know that our bosses approve of our work or think we are doing a good job. And it's always nice to hear when our friends say we are a good friend or parent. Sure, constructive criticism is helpful at times. But again, the problem occurs when we wrap our worth and our sense of who we are into these approvals.

The Vicious Cycle Created by Fear

My once-friend Tara is drop-dead gorgeous, smart, financially fit, and incredibly witty and funny, yet she's one of the most insecure people I've met in my life. She's rarely had a romantic relationship last longer than a few months and thrives on the attention she receives wherever she goes. Even if she is seeing someone, she can't turn down the flirtations and propositions she receives from strangers. If Tara is having a bad day, a second glance and a smile from a stranger in a coffee shop will change her mood completely. Men who get to know her witness her neediness quickly and become tired of her behavior.

Tara's insecurity actually detracts from her physical beauty, dimming a light within. Though initially attracted by her outward beauty, men typically leave Tara after a short time because her insecurity and need for external approval to feel worthy leads her to send relentless text messages, call nonstop, and behave in a very controlling manner. Having men leave her renders Tara feeling even more insecure and rejected, which prompts her to seek new outside attention. It is a relentless and fruitless cycle. She's got so much of her sense of worth tied into her looks.

When we look outside for information about who we are and exercise "object-referral," we are compelled to control things. "We feel an intense need for external power," explains Chopra. "The need for approval, the need to control things, and the need for external power are needs that are based on fear. This kind of power is not the power of pure potentiality, or the power of the Self, or real power. When we experience the power of the Self, there is an absence of fear, there is no compulsion to control, and no struggle for approval or external power."[3]

That's why it's no surprise that Tara's fear-based approach to life led her to be incredibly controlling of others, even friends and coworkers. When you put so much of your power into getting the approval of others, the insecurity makes you crave external control. Controlling others keeps your energy focused on gaining power in the external world, which is not true power. To build real, lasting power, you need to practice self-love, the only true power there is.

The external power that gorgeous, conflicted Tara worked so hard to control causes her so much insecurity because it's unstable, on shaky ground. It's based in fear, causing her enormous anxiety and depression, and it beats up on her physical health. If she could only step back and look *within* for her validation, doing what made *her* feel good for herself, knowing her self-worth because she valued herself, and learned how to tune in to her real power, nurturing her energy within, she could become a much happier person. And perhaps she would finally attract someone who could love her as much as she could love herself.

Resisting the Siren Call of External Validation

Our biggest fear is taking the risk to be alive—the risk to be alive and express who we really are.

—Miguel Ruiz, *The Four Agreements: A Practical Guide to Personal Freedom*

The desire for external validation is a siren call that is very hard to resist. I remember one of the big moments in my life when I had to fight the urge to get external approval about a big decision. As a young adult, I didn't have much of a relationship with either of my parents; neither showed me love, much less showed that they even cared about me. My maternal grandmother was the only person who looked out for me and my best interests and taught me unconditional love.

When I decided to take risks and leave my cushy job for an unsure life as an entrepreneur, you bet my grandmother wasn't pleased. Not because she wanted to see me unhappy but because she worried, and in her experience, people of her generation didn't do risky things to threaten their livelihood. In her mind, I shouldn't leave the security of a steady job with benefits.

I recognized her concern for me and that her opinions about what is "right" to do in my life was not about me but about her lens, her bias and experiences, coming of age during World War II.

I had to work hard to remind myself that what I did was not the same as who I am, and therefore, my actions were not what made my grandmother love or not love me. She was prone to depression and had so much of her sense of worth wrapped up into me, as she always saw me as her personal project. But I couldn't worry about how the decisions I wanted to make for my life would affect her mood or her life. It was my life, and she couldn't live my life for me. Only I could do that; only I knew what was best for me. That's how I was able to stay true to myself. I didn't worry—or at least tried not to—that my grandmother's disapproval meant I was not worthy of her love.

This is not a selfish way of thinking. It is the greatest fact one can learn. I would one day have to realize the same when it came to voicing my approval about my own son's life decisions, which I discuss further in Chapter 19. If I had relied on my grandmother's approval, I would have never left my job, would have gotten married to a certain type of man who looked good on paper, and would never have become a successful entrepreneur.

Validate Yourself!

Basing their value and self-worth on whether they are receiving an award, a promotion, or a shout-out on social media is far too common a practice for people who lack the ability to love themselves.

Can a writer consider herself a writer if all she receives are rejections for publication? If you believe in yourself and your work, rejection won't stop you from continuing on. There are countless stories of now-famous writers and artists who were rejected dozens of times, if not hundreds, before landing their first deal. Is an entrepreneur still an entrepreneur if no patrons enter her storefront? Is a healer still a healer if she has never gone to med school?

The answers depend on whether the person believes they are who they are based on the things they do, the involvement of outsiders, or on what they know about their nature and purpose. The more you try to please others, the less you tune in to yourself and what you love about you. You miss opportunities to put forth your gifts to others, contributing to the world in the manner you were designed to. If you rely on what others think of you to feel good about yourself, you'll focus on doing what pleases others rather than what pleases you.

This is not self-love. You end up creating a false version of yourself that takes a lot of energy to uphold and that you put forth in the world as "you." If you can learn to let go of this false self, this self that is not really you, you'll free up a ton of wasted energy.

When you are in a state of self-love and self-acceptance, you are immune to criticism that comes from someone else's values or beliefs, fears or concerns. You do not back down from any challenge.

So stop evaluating your value based on what other people do or what they say about you. Look inward. Have the strength to do what pleases you, what feels right in your gut. Contribute to the world in the ways that feel right, especially given your own specific gifts. That's how you can start undermining the saboteur of external validation.

JOURNALING SUGGESTION

When Have You Sought Out External Validation?

Write down a current or past situation in which you have taken action in your life based on receiving approval from others. Maybe you decided to major in premed because you come from two generations of oncologists, or said yes to taking your mother to Atlantic City in lieu of a girls' weekend that you really needed, or took a job just for the money rather than the lower-paying one you knew would fulfill you personally.

- Did you gain the approval you sought by making that decision?
- What do you think would have happened if you had chosen to do what would have made you happy instead?

continued

Write down a situation where you didn't receive approval or validation from someone, which left you feeling bad about yourself or maybe even depressed. Perhaps a family member didn't approve of something you were doing, a friend didn't like your new haircut, or your Instagram post didn't get as many likes as you hoped for.

- What did you do in response? Did it change your behavior in any way?
- Can you see how, in these circumstances, you put your power into gaining external approval or even a certain definition of who you are as a person, rather than look within to examine how you view yourself, your values, and your actions?

As long as what you are doing makes you feel good, you will live a life full of joy, peace, and love.

Chapter 6

Allowing Social Conditioning and Programming to Guide Your Behavior

The way we were brought up, generational ideas and traditions, expectations of parents or other authority figures, past experiences, mistakes we watched people make—such things influence how we are conditioned and programmed to live in the world and how we view ourselves. Like the dogs that learned to salivate at the ringing of Pavlov's bell, our responses are shaped by the relationships and situations we encounter in our lives. The trouble is, those automatic responses can stand in the way of practicing self-love.

Social Conditioning Starts Young

First and foremost, we are programmed by our parents. Some people might look back and repeat the patterns purposefully, believing the way they were raised made sense. Others might look back on a past riddled with flaws and dysfunction and do everything in their power to do the opposite. The issue with the latter is that regardless of whether we consciously set out to create a world completely different from our past, we are still conditioned by it.

For instance, having had a mentally abusive mother who would lash out at me in written form, usually via a letter or email, I made sure to instead verbally communicate in a healthy way with my son, keeping an open channel of communication with no judgment of his point of view.

Even though I chose to never mirror my mother's behavior, I would come to learn that I was still tethered to conditioning that resulted from her behavior toward me. Through trauma work, including some of the self-help work I did while reading Mastin Kipp's book titled *Claim Your Power*, I was shocked to discover that I had formed all kinds of beliefs about myself as a result of the abuse. I really had no idea beliefs such as "I'm not lovable," "I am all alone in this world," and "I can't be vulnerable" were programmed into my subconscious during this time in my life. These beliefs (a.k.a. limiting beliefs, which I discuss in Chapter 11) formed toxic relationship patterns that I wasn't able to move on from until I uncovered them, worked to heal them (and I'm still working!), and began forming new and healthier beliefs to replace them.

Social conditioning has many other influences as well. Society has us, as women, fall into certain roles that would be considered more female. Both males and females come into the world in tune with their emotions. Little boys cry just like little girls do. In his world-renowned book *The Four Agreements*, Miguel Ruiz describes his interpretation of how conditioning and programming happen. "Children believe everything adults say. We agree with them, and our faith is so strong that the belief system controls our whole dream of life. We didn't choose these beliefs, and we may have rebelled against them, but we were not strong enough to win the rebellion. The result is surrender to the beliefs with our agreement."[1]

Ruiz calls this process the "domestication of humans." It is the process of being told how to live, the meanings of people and things: mom, dad, milk, fork. "The outside dream teaches us how to be human. We have a whole concept of what a 'woman' is and what a 'man' is. And we also learned to judge: we judge ourselves, judge other people, judge the neighbors."[2]

Young boys are taught by their parents and everyone around them that being a real man means they aren't allowed to show emotion; it's young girls (who become women) who are "emotional." Men don't cry, and if they do, they are accused of acting "like a girl." If there's a man in the boy's life, he sees it as his job to teach that boy "how to be a man." It's all part of programming and conditioning.

The opposite scenario is true. If a girl doesn't cry, she is "cold"; if she is assertive, she is a bitch. And so society encourages girls to stay in touch with their emotions and boys to squelch them. These social constructs work to control us all. Staying in the lanes our programming has determined for us—whether focused on gender, sex, race, socioeconomic status, or an identity like sinner or saint—keeps us distant and unacquainted with our true selves. Writes Ruiz, "We pretend to be what we are not because we are afraid of being rejected. The fear of being rejected becomes the fear of not being good enough. Eventually we become someone that we are not. We become a copy of Mamma's beliefs, Daddy's beliefs, society's beliefs, and religion's beliefs."[3]

> Staying in the lanes our programming has determined for us keeps us distant and unacquainted with our true selves.

Social Conditioning Never Stops!

It's difficult to understand exactly where conditioning or programming begins. But sometimes it is just "the way things have always been," or the roles we saw our mothers play or a mistake that had negative consequences that caused us to become risk averse. The ways we are conditioned are limitless. What is important to note is that even in adulthood we are programmed by those

continued

around us. Women who speak up at work are "bitches," so we start to play it small. Or it's okay for a child's father to miss the school concert because of work, but not for the mother, so she often takes off work and then finds she doesn't get invited to important meetings in the office.

Conditioning Is a Harsh Judge

We've learned to place value on judging ourselves and others. We label things as right or wrong, good or bad. These learned systems of labeling as good/bad or right/wrong are part of our social conditioning—taught to us by our parents, society, school, peers, communities, and religions, and then programmed into our brains. At first, we are taught by others, rewarded for behaviors seen as good, and punished for behaviors judged as bad. Then pretty soon, as we grow into adulthood, we get good at judging ourselves and keeping ourselves in line.

Succumbing to the judge of conditioning leads us to become someone we are not and does not allow any opportunity to know ourselves and therefore find love for ourselves. When we don't follow what is expected, we punish ourselves. Ruiz says humans judge everything—the weather, our pets, the things we want to purchase, everything we do and don't do, everything we think and don't think, and everything we feel and don't feel. "Everything lives under the tyranny of this judge," he writes. "Every time we do something that goes against the Book of Law, the Judge says we are guilty, we need to be punished, we should be ashamed. This happens many times a day, day after day, for all the years of our lives."[4]

But this system of judging things and people as good or bad, right or wrong, is what keeps us from our true power, and keeps us disconnected from each other and the universe. On the other side of our human existence, at the level of the soul, there is no judgment, only unconditional love. As Deepak Chopra explains in a LinkedIn blog post, "There's a reason . . . the spiritual side of our nature is attracted to nonjudgment. We want to love and be loved. At a deeper level, we realize that all suffering is ultimately related to self-judgment."[5]

It is obvious that judging ourselves based on the standards of society, our family, our friends, or whoever is the opposite of self-love. We get stuck in a life pattern shaped by beliefs that are not our own. Constant self-criticism invokes a sense of self that feels shameful, victimized, blamed, guilty. We say, "Poor me, I'm not good enough. I'm not intelligent enough. I'm not attractive enough. I'm not worthy of love." Perhaps worse still, we hold back our true selves, hiding whatever we think won't be approved of by others.

We've learned to let our guilt and shame mechanisms override the need to look out for ourselves first and foremost. We've let guilt take on a life of its own, letting it talk us out of putting our needs and our happiness first.

That all has to change. Starting now. Stop the self-sabotage! Stop judging yourself as unworthy if you fail to live up to an expectation that society has placed on you. Believe you are worthy because you exist. Give yourself a break, especially as you start the hard work of changing your thinking to be less critical and more supportive of your value as a human being.

As mentioned earlier, I learned a lot from author Anita Moorjani, best-selling author of Dying to Be Me, who had a near-death experience after being in a coma for thirty hours. During this period of "clarity," as she describes it, she could "see my own magnificence undistorted by fear." She realized that she had, in her words, "never loved myself, valued myself, or seen the beauty of my own soul." Now, she tries to live how the universe intends her live, "without needing to change. . . . I don't have to try to live up to other people's expectations of perfection and then feel inadequate when I fail miserably. . . . I [don't] have to try to become someone else in order to be worthy. We just have to be true to ourselves and become instruments of loving energy."[6]

I couldn't have said it better.

What Has Your Upbringing Conditioned You to Expect from Your Life?

The most challenging part of social conditioning is that we learn to take certain things for granted, as the way life should turn out. Sometimes, it's very difficult to tease out the parts of our lives that are based on our individual choices and those based on what society has laid out for us.

As a journal exercise, pick one area of your life—job/career, family, friends, romantic partner/spouse, hobbies, health/fitness, or anything else you'd like to explore.

- Brainstorm what expectations you have in that area. And remember that there is *no editing* when you're brainstorming! Just jot down anything that comes to mind about what you think you should be doing or accomplishing in that area.

- Then review your list and challenge yourself about whether that expectation is based on your own dreams and desires or on something that family, friends, or society says you should be doing.

Chapter 7

Letting Guilt Override You

What is guilt anyway? As discussed in the previous chapter, judgment is a learned human behavior. Guilt is a response to the judge. When you feel guilty, you're making a judgment that *something you've done* is wrong. (Guilt, by the way, often gets confused with its cousin shame, which is when you make a judgment that what's wrong is *you*, rather than what you did.) Guilt is fabricated inside the mind and then given energy by you *if* you choose to give it that energy.

Guilt Made Me Do It

It wasn't until my last breakup that I had a big epiphany about the controlling forces of guilt. Had I given in to these forces, it would have kept me stuck in a relationship that wasn't benefiting me and would have held me back from major personal growth.

My on-and-off boyfriend, Dave, and I had gotten into a conflict one night. I was voicing my concerns about the fact that I didn't feel like he valued me or was concerned at all with putting any effort into being a good partner. We had recently moved in together, and I already felt as though I was doing all the work to ensure that we were working toward the common goal of building a life together. I could tell my power container was reaching dangerously low levels.

During our tense discussion, Dave told me he wasn't capable of meeting my needs.

"Of course you're capable," I said. "You just have to want to try."

I had been feeling so depleted, trying to make the relationship work from my end, trying to please him and help him, that I didn't have the focus or energy to work on the new business I was trying to build. I didn't feel like myself; I was depressed and dissatisfied. I withdrew from social activities and didn't keep up with friends. At the same time, I felt overwhelming love for this man, as if somehow he was my responsibility. But I was sacrificing myself, my energy level, my progress, and my happiness in order to constantly exhibit my love for him.

We took a couple of days to have some space apart, and still I hadn't come to any specific conclusions other than the instinct that things weren't right despite my love for him. Again, Dave told me he was unsure he had the capability to meet my needs. Then he asked me, "Do you think I'm capable?"

"Of course I think you're capable," I answered, when I really should've said, "No" (see more on the word "no" later). Instead, I thought to myself, *How could he not be capable? How hard is it to occasionally stop to give your girlfriend a little love and appreciation? How difficult is it not to drink so often so that you can be present and fully engaged in a conversation and give a little attention to your girlfriend? It just takes a conscious effort. This should not be such a difficult thing to do.*

Dave put the burden on me to answer the question and then went a step further and asked me to help him be capable. Help him not drink so much, help him be more of what I needed him to be, help him see my value. At the time, I didn't realize it was just more of him relying on me to keep the energy of our relationship going.

While it felt like we talked through it, whatever "it" was, I still felt unsettled and unhappy while trying to sleep. I played back our make-up session on the couch when Dave turned to me and said, "You are so pretty," which caused me to unexpectedly weep.

"Do you know, I think that is the second time you have ever said that to me in the entire time we've been together?" I said to him, surprised by my own vulnerable response.

He paused, watching me wipe my tears, and gave me a solemn look before answering bluntly, "You deserve better than that, Jenna."

"You're right, I do."

If that were the case, then why was I still lying in bed with this man, pretending that miraculously overnight we'd turn into a couple on the same path, pretending my job would be to make him a better man, a better partner? I was exhausted already, and the night hadn't even ended yet. He quickly fell right asleep, while I tossed and turned. My instinct just kept telling me to get out of this relationship now. He wasn't capable of meeting my needs, and I had too much I wanted to do in life to waste time trying to singlehandedly keep a relationship strong.

Why was loving him not enough? Why was the relationship making me feel so damn bad? I fought the guilty feelings of what might happen if I *did* help him. Surely, I owed it to him to try even harder, stay loyal, and keep my promise to help him "be capable," didn't I? That guilty voice was no stranger to me.

The thing about guilt is it's not necessarily a bad emotion. Feeling it might mean you know you're doing something, or have done something, that goes against your moral code. What was I so guilty of? I could rattle off the list of what I thought my responsibilities were to him and how leaving would somehow shirk those responsibilities, but that wasn't my truth. I thought intensely about how I was willing to treat him—all the continued effort and attention, not to mention the free business work, home help, and financial help I'd offer, along with helping him reverse some of his unhealthy behaviors and habits. Then, I thought, *What if Jenna was going to do all of that and more for Jenna?* When I thought about shifting energy from him to me, about loving myself more than I was loving him, I started to see the guilt as unwarranted—irrational even—and it became easier for me to say goodbye to it. By pushing the voice of guilt down, I made space for self-love to remind me not only that I should get out and save myself but also that it was my divine duty to make my life worth much more than it was in that moment.

When I told Dave the next day that I was leaving the relationship, he didn't fight for me. He didn't even try to talk me out of it. This showed me how much he didn't value me, which aligned with the lack of value I had been feeling from him all along.

When Guilt Becomes Resentment

One of my friends and I were talking about exactly this subject one day. She had been feeling resentment toward her boyfriend. She was going through the exact same situation I went through, where she was always bending over backward to help her boyfriend with his life. Yet she felt like she had to pull teeth or get upset with him to get any help around her house or with any of her tasks.

Recently, she made plans to go to lunch and shop with a friend. When her boyfriend unexpectedly told her that he was going to stay at her house that evening, she became stressed and even contemplated cancelling her plans with her friend out of guilt that her boyfriend would be home all alone. She was also worried that she wouldn't be there to cook dinner for him.

But she also knew she'd feel guilty for cancelling plans on her friend, so she opted to keep her plans. The entire time, she felt guilty for not being home with her boyfriend. She wasn't present with her friend, checking her phone incessantly and wondering what her boyfriend was thinking of her. She cut the visit short and went home.

Together we examined that feeling of guilt and where that was coming from. Something in her nature believed she needed to perform certain duties as a woman, regardless of her boyfriend not having such expectations. (See Chapter 6, on social conditioning.)

We act on this deeply embedded conditioning to feel guilty when we do what makes us happy because "it's how we feel," like an itch we can't help scratch because the feeling is so strong. But are these feelings that we have, this instinctual drive to invest so much of ourselves into others, valid? Or could they be holding us back from evolving and taking our rightful place in this world as fully empowered women? As therapist and author Dr. Nae says in a post on her Instagram page, "Guilt keeps you in the status quo. Guilt is not an indication that you made the wrong decision. Just the opposite! Guilt is an indication that we are going against our habitual pattern. Just because it feels bad does not mean it is bad."[1]

Any self-assured and self-aware man today would tell you they can absolutely figure out dinner for themselves. They can also get their houses in order and take care of their needs—just like we women can for ourselves. There are delivery apps, restaurants, people you can hire to clean and complete tasks for you at home. And I can assure you that these men would still love you, just as my friend found with her boyfriend. In fact, he'd probably love you even more if you put your own needs as higher priorities and stopped trying to please others all the time. Especially if by trying to please them, you end up unhappy and unfulfilled when you don't get the same in return.

Yet we continue to give and give of ourselves, not getting enough back, causing us to become depleted and drained of our vital energy. How can we be the best versions of ourselves when we're so depleted and don't even bother to question the very nature of what causes this depletion in the first place?

I gave my friend an idea to try to help her work through her feelings of guilt when a situation like that arises again so that she can get back to enjoying herself, her day, and her friend. The next time, she should take out her phone, open the notes section, and write down the following question: "What are the consequences of not being home for my boyfriend?"

She imagined her answer would be, "He would have to figure out his own dinner. He would do what he would normally do—get on his computer, watch TV, play a game on his phone. He wouldn't bat an eyelash." All those answers quickly offset any guilty feeling because she proved that her guilt was simply coming from inside herself, a narrative she was telling herself—and there it was in black and white.

No Guilt in Choosing Yourself

Let's say you decided to practice some self-care and take off an evening after work to enjoy some relaxation at the local day spa. You've got two young kids at home, and you've asked your husband to feed the kids dinner, help them with their homework, and get them ready for bed so you can decompress. You could choose to feel guilty about taking some much-needed self-care time and let that prevent you from actually enjoying your down time. Or you could choose not to feel guilty and choose yourself.

Whatever choice you make for yourself also affects those around you. If you choose not to feel guilty, then your husband will have to accept the fact that this is something you really need, and he should support you in that decision. But if you feel any fear about how he might feel about your choice to care for yourself, or guilt that you're not there sacrificing yourself and your needs for your kids or husband, then that energy will reflect back to you when you get home. You will get feedback or reinforcement of how you feel based on your energy.

If you take the opportunity to pour some much-needed love from yourself onto yourself, without fear or guilt, you are coming from a place of true love. And that love will be reflected back to you when you get home because your energy will be full of love. Your family will see the difference in you and will be happy to show you even more of that beautiful love that you've just given yourself. Your kids will get by just fine without you for one evening. What you choose to believe becomes your reality. It *is* a choice.

I may feel guilt about something, but I've learned I can observe that feeling of guilt as separate, and instead tune in to my intuition (that feeling of happiness or discomfort) that may be guiding me to make a different decision (based on what best serves me) than my guilt might make for me. (See also Chapter 9, on ignoring our intuition.)

JOURNALING SUGGESTION

What Do You Feel Guilty About?

Write down any time recently when you may have felt guilty about wanting to do something for yourself.

- Why did you feel guilty about it?
- How could you have approached this situation differently despite the guilty feeling?

Chapter 8

Relying on False Hope

Will you take that phony dream and burn it
before something happens?
—Arthur Miller, *Death of a Salesman*

Hope is said to be one of the most beneficial drivers of motivation, resilience, and satisfaction. But for those of us who are floundering without self-love, hope can act like quicksand, sinking us deeper into the murkiness of insecurity, uncertainty, and regret. Hope can become false hope when we attach ourselves to the image a person presents. And that false hope can make it even harder to seize our value and power. Once again, I speak from experience.

Strangled by Hope

Despite the fact that it was my decision to break it off with Dave, I hadn't experienced heartbreak like that before. I loved this man deeply and losing him left a hole in my heart and a void in my life. As much as I tried to move forward and create a life without him, I have to be honest and admit I held on to hope at first as a way to get me through the initial pain. All it took to keep me tethered to him was an open channel of connection in the form of him sending a random text every now and again. Usually, it was a question or suggestion about something logistical, like "Who did you use to waterproof your basement?" or "Can I get my table out of your shed?" He would use the opportunity to then ask, "How have you been?" or "What have you been up to?" Benign things like that, when you are secretly holding on to hope, can feel like they mean much more. Every time he'd do that, I'd engage and read into it, and it would throw my progress into a tailspin. My head would swim with "what ifs" and the hope that somehow he'd come around and see that he missed me or somehow realized how much he valued me.

Each text message from Dave fueled this false hope, believing as I did that it meant he was interested in my life, which I interpreted as interest in me. *He is inquiring; therefore, he must realize what he lost and just doesn't know how to voice it.* Just writing those words now, seeing how my false hope gave my power over to him, irks me to my core. As discussed in the introduction, giving your power away is the opposite of loving yourself.

But I worked hard to stay strong and analyze these feelings that came up. One day, I asked myself, *Why do I have this undying hope that he'll come around? Why would he suddenly become someone different than he's always been?* I was addicted to the feeling I had from when we first started dating and how he treated me early on. He gave me a glimpse of something I wanted. If he'd already acted in ways that showed he valued me, my hope was he would reprise them in the future. He was certainly capable of doing something he had already done. I had to realize over time that those actions of our early courtship were never based in reality.

I realized that my unrelenting false hope would keep me from moving on and putting myself first and the relationship behind me, even after I left it. It was a real battle to fight my natural emotional drive to keep this hope alive, juxtaposed with my logical senses that told me he wasn't capable of being the person I needed him to be.

Breaking Free from False Hope

My own strategy for breaking free from the false hope that had trapped me was to begin writing down in my journal an inventory of my relationship values in one column, ranking them in order of importance (see Chapter 23 for a partial list of relationship values). In another column, I ranked on a scale of 1–10 how well Dave met those values. Each answer I wrote down ranked somewhere in the range of 1–3. This simple exercise was incredibly helpful in allowing me to see empirically that no amount of hope, false or otherwise, would make this man capable of giving me what I needed. There it was in ink; he truly was incapable of meeting my needs in a relationship.

Whenever that feeling of hope would creep back up—and boy did it—I'd review this journal entry. What a wonderful thing for me to see, like pouring water on a fire. During this time, I began to contemplate why I was compelled to help him as if his life were my responsibility. Somehow I felt if I had the ability or skills to help, even in areas of his life where he did not ask me to help him, it was my duty. For instance, right at the end of our breakup conversation, I told him that I'd still get his marketing project done for him, a project I hadn't even started. He didn't ask me to do that, but somehow making that promise made me feel—you guessed it—less guilty!

I was talking with a friend not long after I recognized this "false hope" conditioning that I had been battling. She quickly made the correlation to her own marriage. The same problems they were now dealing with as a married couple many years into their relationship were the exact same problems they had when they were dating.

He was definitely incapable of meeting her needs as she had envisioned. Yet somehow she always had hope that he would and always believed that he was capable somewhere deep within. In her mind, if he'd only come to realize how much he valued her and the relationship, he would meet her needs, and all would be perfect in their relationship.

They broke up while dating, and she, like me, held out hope that somehow he'd come around and see the light. But unlike me, she gave in to her hope, got back together, and married this man. And in the end, nothing changed. Now she was at a point where she had lost any hope that even therapy would be able to help them. She realized her hope, the same hope that I had, the kind that hangs on to the idea of a person instead of who that person really is, was driving their relationship all along.

For some time, she had been putting so much of herself into her husband and marriage, hoping he would in turn provide her with what she needed to sustain her energy output. But she was now worn thin and realized something had to change. I asked her to try to focus some of her energy during the day on her self-care instead of putting her own self-care needs aside as she had been. She had stopped doing all the things, small things, for herself that made her happy, such as getting massages, having her hair done, spending time with friends, focusing on self-development. She had put all her love needs into one basket, and not the basket that really counted—hers. How can someone expect to be shown love when she is not showing love to herself? This brings me back to that old but valid phrase: *You have to love yourself first in order to let someone love you.*

And what if instead of hoping that he would meet her needs, and then getting constantly upset with him when he didn't, my friend accepted her husband for who he is, along with the fact that he wasn't going to change? And what if she turned some of that energy toward looking within and examining where this feeling of hope was coming from? Could she get to the source? Chances are her hope was based not on any sort of logic but on deeply embedded conditioning.

I pointed out that giving up false hope would free up wasted negative energy that she could use in more positive ways. And perhaps rather than putting so much hope into her husband to be something he's not, she could put her faith in herself, her capabilities, her happiness. The newfound relief might create a new, more realistic basis to work from, whether or not she decides to stay in the relationship.

Since our conversation, I've seen many positive changes in my friend. She is now doing things that make her happy again, taking responsibility for her own happiness rather than focusing so much of her energy trying to get her husband to change and to make her happy. She's gone back to spending more time with her friends and family, practicing self-care, and doing things that enrich and grow her, guilt free. In my opinion, because she is now doing the things that make her happy, as well as releasing the negative energy of false hope that she had, the energy in her relationship has turned more positive. Who knows—they may even pull through because of her shift in attitude and expectations.

JOURNALING SUGGESTION

How Has False Hope Influenced Your Life?

Write down a past experience when you may have experienced similar false hope. How did this false hope affect your behavior?

Chapter 9

Ignoring Your Intuition

Intuition is a sense of knowing how to act spontaneously,
without needing to know why.
—Sylvia Clare, *Trusting Your Intuition*

When you grow up with a lot of negativity, trauma, neglect, and dysfunction, it takes a toll on your psyche—and your body. I would experience intense feelings deep in the center of my body, tingling sensations when a stranger was near, or a heavy, negative vibe if I sensed someone had bad intentions. When danger or negativity was around me, or I was making wrong choices and hanging with the wrong people, I'd experience debilitating dips in my energy level. On the bright side, experiencing prolonged physical sensations such as these helped me make certain connections and correlations. I'd notice that these symptoms would happen in circumstances that didn't suit me, and at a young age, I began to understand that I didn't need to rely on logic or intellect to make pragmatic decisions about things that were good and bad for me; it was okay to just trust my gut because these feelings were to be trusted.

Call it instinct, intuition, or just going with your gut, understanding that we are capable of making key decisions in direct and instant ways is something that has been deemed "woo-woo" by many. We believe (thanks to programming and conditioning) that to make solid decisions or come to the "right" conclusions, we should burn our brains by thinking and deliberating. We only trust conscious decision-making. But there are times when quick judgments and our first impressions offer more apt ways of staying true to ourselves. Your spirit knows what you need, and that energy found in your solar plexus (about two fingers above your belly button) speaks to you daily; when you don't listen to it, you tell yourself you are not worth listening to—and that is not self-love. There is a reason your gut is dubbed the "powerhouse." When we don't use it, we lose energy and we lose power, which is why the first telltale sign of me ignoring my intuition is lack of energy to the point of debilitating fatigue.

The Power of Intuitive Thinking

While psychics and spiritual healers are very much credited with busting open the topic of intuition, more and more intuition is being recognized as mainstream, with even the most level-headed white coats getting on board in their research labs.

For example, in his groundbreaking book *Blink: The Power of Thinking without Thinking*, Malcolm Gladwell legitimizes intuitive thinking, which is known by some researchers as "unconscious thinking." It operates below the surface of consciousness. Gladwell writes that unconscious thinking "sends its messages through weirdly indirect channels, such as the sweat glands in the palms of our hands. It's a system in which our brain reaches conclusions without immediately telling us that it's reaching conclusions."[1]

Gladwell continues, "The only way that human beings could have ever survived as a species for as long as we have is that we've developed another kind of decision-making apparatus that is capable of making very quick judgments based on very little information."[2]

According to the theory of unconscious decision-making, we use a second part of our brain whenever we meet a new person, are

interviewed for a new job, hear a new idea, are faced with a big decision under stress, are in a relationship that is becoming more serious,
and so on. What Gladwell really set out to uncover is not necessarily
how or why we have intuition but why we choose to purposely ignore
it. Why do we ignore those crazy signals that flood our entire bodies?
Why does a woman say yes to a marriage proposal even though hearing
the words makes her want to vomit? Why does someone let a solicitor
through the front door, even though their red flags are waving like mad?
Why, despite a new coworker giving off negative or sinister vibes, does
a person offer their proprietary ideas, only to have them stolen?

   "Our instinctive reactions often have to compete with all kinds of
other interests and emotions and sentiments," writes Gladwell.[3] We
talked about false hope already, which is one of the reasons we turn
away from our gut. *We simply really, really want this to be true.* Other
reasons include denial, a sense of attachment or sentiment, and bias.

Learning to Trust Intuition

I learned to trust my intuition implicitly, because I had to as a young
person with little parental guidance. I had to find a compass somehow,
and it wound up being my
inner one. In that way, I feel
some gratitude toward my
parents. They forced me into
a life in which, out of sheer
necessity for survival, I had
nothing other than my gut to
guide me, and to this day, it
has never misguided me.

> I learned to trust my
> intuition implicitly, because
> I had to as a young person
> with little parental guidance.

   I recognized a pattern where I would have an instinct, a tiny little voice, that whispered to me when I had to make a decision about
something. And I distinctly remember those times I second-guessed

that little voice and instead would "think myself" into making a more deliberate decision. When I looked back at those times when I let thinking overpower my intuition, I could see that my intuition turned out to be correct. So each time that I did not trust my instincts, I would end up making the wrong decision. For me now, it's second nature to resist overthinking and instead to pay attention to those feelings in my body. Even when I'm making high-stakes, life-changing decisions, if my instinct is clearly telling me something, I always follow it, even if it doesn't make logical sense at the time. Let me be clear though, for many people the physical signals can be subtle. Perhaps many people ignore their instincts precisely because they are so subtle.

Many years ago, I had been working for a company for quite a while. While the job was initially exciting and challenging, with independence, resources, a team, and unlimited monetary growth potential, the job eventually became tedious and sucked the life out of me. However, the six-figure income and very nice benefit package kept me in those so-called golden handcuffs.

Lifeless and yearning for more, I woke up day after day wondering what was wrong with me, why I had low-grade depression and felt stuck. I knew my power container was not even close to full. Yet I told myself it would be ridiculous to quit this job, and so I didn't.

We had hired a new salesperson in our department on a temporary contract. I started realizing she was a bit of a bad seed. The executive team and I decided to not renew her temporary contract. I remember going into the office a few days before her contract expired and feeling this intense negative vibration in my body. It felt personal, like it was directed at me, like I was under some kind of attack. I just didn't want to be there, and I trusted that feeling 100 percent, so I abruptly left.

Now explain that to your boss. As odd as I knew it would sound, I was honest, telling him I sensed I was being threatened and trusted my instinct to remove myself from the room. I called him from my car on my way home. He demanded that I come back, which upset me more because I'd been a very good, loyal employee—not to mention I had made them many millions during my tenure there. I told him I would not come back as long as this person was physically in the office. This was about me and my safety. It was about me trusting my instincts 100 percent and trusting that it was for my own benefit in the end. If my boss wasn't going to look out for my well-being, I had to do it myself, regardless of the consequences.

While I was home, I decided it was time to hand in my resignation and move on. I really just didn't want to be at that job anymore, especially if I wasn't being supported by my boss. That salesperson was let go by one of the executive managers without incident during my few days away.

Citing "insubordination," my boss reprimanded me in his office upon my return. Already having decided to quit, I handed in my two-weeks' notice, which I believe caught him off guard. He probably thought those golden handcuffs were on pretty tight.

A few days later, I was chatting with the gentleman who manned the front desk. He casually mentioned to me that the temporary salesperson who had been let go told him a few days before her last day that she knew she was going down and that she was going to take "a couple of bitches down with her." Based on the negative energy that I felt that day from her, I'd say she was going to ensure that she wreaked havoc on my life. I wasn't surprised at all. It made everything that I'd felt and noticed make sense and made me further realize that my instinct definitely had my best interest at heart. I felt the universe was pushing me out of a nest that I instinctively knew I had grown out of a long time ago.

Once my boss learned of this incident with the front desk person, he immediately backpedaled. He, along with a couple other members of executive management, took me to lunch, told me they would love to have me stay, and offered me my job back, even though I'd already found them a great replacement for my position.

I had been feeling good about the decision to leave, springing up in the morning without dread, fueled with creativity about what I planned to do next. Those were also instincts telling me I was on the right path. I had been charging my power container back up by following my instincts and it felt great! Nothing they did or said could have made me stay. It wasn't about any "I told you so" (an external power, which isn't real power anyway), and it wasn't about having some kind of upper hand or "control" of the situation. It was about me trusting my instinct that it was time to change and do other things in my life.

If I had never quit, I might never have eventually gone on to pursue my entrepreneurial endeavors. I probably would still be stuck in my little rent-controlled, run-down apartment, just making enough to get by in California, even with a six-figure income. I later went on to buy two rental properties in Atlanta and sold a home-based company I founded for $500,000. I wouldn't have been able to travel all over the world with all the new friends I made after moving across the country to a more affordable city. If I had ignored my intuition, I wouldn't have been able to experience the freedom and fulfillment that come from being my own boss and growing a company.

Tuning In to Your Intuition

How do you know when your instinct is giving you guidance? It can come in the form of a hunch, a sensation that something feels off or doesn't feel right. Or it could be a strong urge. These feelings are there for a reason, to guide and support you. We have to learn not to ignore them.

The more you decide to tune in to your intuition and go with it, the more you'll see for yourself that those hunches are right. In my experience, the proof that my action is right doesn't always immediately appear, but eventually the truth reveals itself, and I learn my intuition-based choices are right for me. Try it yourself. Be patient. You'll come to trust your intuition because you'll realize it's always right.

JOURNALING SUGGESTION

Tune In to Your Intuition

Write down a situation in the past where you had a hunch or a gut feeling about something, but you let your logic stop you from acting on that feeling, and your hunch turned out to be right. It could be something as simple as not grabbing an umbrella when you had a gut feeling that you needed to grab one. Or maybe it's something bigger like feeling a sense of danger, but you didn't act on that and something bad happened.

What do you think would have happened if you had trusted your intuition instead and taken action based on that gut feeling?

Chapter 10

Never Saying No

Every time you say yes to something you don't want to do, this will happen: you will resent people, you will do a bad job, you will have less energy for the things you were doing a good job on, you will make less money, and yet another small percentage of your life will be burned up.
—James Altucher, *Choose Yourself*

One of the shortest words the English language—heck, in pretty much all languages—is "no." It's so easy to say that, for many a toddler, the word "no" is notoriously the first word uttered. ("Mine" is another. If only girls and women could defend their turf in the way a toddler can!) Instead, one of the only times women know how to say the word "no" is when they say no to saying no. That is, we don't want to tell someone, anyone no, so we say yes. When that happens, we are effectively saying, "My time and energy are not mine; they're yours." We need to channel our inner toddler. Let's put "no" back into your vocabulary.

Avoiding No

Sure, okay, why not, it's fine. These are the answers we give when we want to say no. But have you noticed they aren't exactly saying yes either? This is the space of ambivalence women put themselves into, agreeing to things, because being agreeable is what we've been taught to be. "What's mine is yours," even if it means our life. *That's a nice girl.*

Each one of the previous saboteurs I've discussed add up to why we fail to say no. We have been living with expectations for most of our lives—expectations that if we say yes and do more, we will be "good enough." What will happen if we push back? First, let me tell you how it feels when we don't: like a betrayal of self that sends a message that we don't love ourselves enough to defend our own honor, time, talents, resources, gifts, goals, spirit, and love for others. Guilty. As. Charged.

I had decided to start dating again after taking a long break. (If you have ever been subjected to the dating scene, you get why a break was necessary!) I met a doctor through a dating app and agreed to meet for a drink. As a confident, secure, empowered woman, I can be a bit intimidating to some men, especially if they aren't used to being around women like me or if they are already insecure. The doctor's shaky hands and fumbling and overly long answers to my small-talk questions proved him to be nervous and uncomfortable. Not being one to try to have any power over other people, I quickly tried to make him feel comfortable by being warm, friendly, and open.

Within the hour, after a second round of drinks, Dr. Quiet was inching his bar stool closer to mine. Then, *Is that a hand on the small of my back?* I shuffled away; he took the hint for a brief time, and then he picked right up where he left off. *Is he touching my leg?*

He wasn't being gross or naughty, but his lack of boundaries was a turnoff and a red flag. How could a grown woman with a previous marriage and a number of long-term relationships behind her, multiple businesses, an adult child, and a successful career (that would be me) find it so difficult to tell this man no to his advances? Because that's what happened. I let it continue. I had a fear of making things uncomfortable, so keeping my mouth shut was how I could avoid confrontation or making him feel stupid. After all, I'd already taken on the role of not making him feel uncomfortable. After the date ended, I felt icky. Icky about him, but to a larger degree, disappointed with myself. What really was the worst thing that could've happened if I had politely but firmly told him to stop his encroachment because it made me uncomfortable?

Either he would've listened and apologized, which would have been redeeming, or he wouldn't have listened, which would have certified him as a jerk, and a good thing I found out sooner rather than later. Either way I looked at it, only good things would have resulted. Saying no would have been an act of self-love.

But I let myself down. Instead, right away I blocked his number on my phone, which was not as empowering as saying an actual no. But at least I immediately took my power back and avoided having to deal with further disempowering behavior. But it's much better to say no than to suffer the consequences of not saying no. Therapists cite the following consequences of not saying no to the things we don't want to do: poor friendships based on feeling resentment or manipulation, depression, anxiety, lack of personal identity, divorce and breakups, stress, and burnout.

Karma's a B

Far too many times I've been guilty of—or have friends who are guilty of—using karma as a reason to say yes all the time. We want good juju, as they say, and good deeds will be repaid. If not, watch out, because karma's a bitch.

Except, if your spirit isn't fully on board, saying yes to things you want to say no to puts negativity out in the world. Your secret resentment or anger or inconvenience tells the universe all you are is a big fat liar. And that is no path to a rewarding life.

Karma is simply the energy you put out, which then returns to you in kind. If the energy behind what you're doing isn't an honest yes, then really, you're just saying no, whether or not you do the task. And there is no good karmic benefit from doing something you don't want to do. In fact, you'll be generating the opposite type of karma that you were hoping to get by doing a task that you really don't want to do. You're being much more honest and caring to yourself and to others when you say no when you feel like it. In fact, it is showing love to yourself when you take care of yourself and your needs first.

The Importance of No

Seemingly small moments in which you don't stand up for yourself and your best interests, where you settle for something that makes you feel bad rather than feel good, slowly chip away at your feeling of self-worth and self-love. There is no such thing as a small moment. They all matter.

The friend who asks you for a lift to the airport.

Your sister who asks you to babysit all the time.

A party you know you will not have fun at.

Making coffee at work when ten guys are completely capable of making coffee themselves.

When at the end of my relationship with my ex-boyfriend Dave, he asked me, "Do you think I am capable?" and my first answer that night was an immediate and almost-reflexive yes, I decided to take a different approach and responded the next morning with the painful but more empowered answer. I said, "No, I do not think you're capable." That no would come to inject more power, energy, and love in my life (I'm talking here about self-love) than I've ever felt before.

So just say no. It's okay. No one is going to hold it against you. Even Dave wasn't making a stink once I finally got the word out. If you've been a doormat for others in the past, when you start standing up for yourself and do what you want to do, others will learn to treat you with more respect. Your friend will download the Lyft app or call another friend for a ride; your sister will ask another relative for help with the kids; the party will go on; one of the men in the office will make a fresh pot of coffee or suffer through caffeine withdrawal at their own hands. This, of course, is assuming you would prefer to spend your time doing something else rather than doing these things for someone else. Of course, I love helping others, as most of us do. I'm not saying that you shouldn't help others. But if you feel like saying no in certain situations, it's always best for you to go with that feeling. That's just you looking out for your best interests; you are being loving to yourself first. And that's self-love.

JOURNALING SUGGESTION

When Have You Said Yes but Wanted to Say No?

Think back to the last time you said yes to something even though you wanted to say no.

- Briefly describe the situation.
- What made you want to say no?
- Why did you say yes anyway?
- If a similar situation arises again, what could you do differently?
  If you want to say no, what would you feel comfortable saying to decline the request? (It may be as simple as saying, "Unfortunately, I can't." And no made-up excuses are necessary.)

Chapter 11

Having Self-Limiting Beliefs

Potential underutilized leads to pain.
—Attributed to Jim Rohn

I'm cursed with bad luck. I will never be loved. I'm not educated enough to have a good career. Love always ends in pain. I'm not worthy of anything better.

These statements we repeat to ourselves over and over are self-limiting beliefs. A *self-limiting* belief is something we believe to be true that limits what we think we deserve or can achieve in life; it keeps us from achieving our potential and keeps us stuck in certain behavior patterns.

Most of the time self-limiting beliefs have been subconsciously programmed into our brain from previous experiences, from our peers, parents, or other authority figures. But just because you believe something to be true doesn't have to make it true for the rest of your life.

While writing this book, for example, I discovered that I had a limiting belief that I suck at writing. Once I became aware of it, I realized that I've had this belief for as long as I can remember. So I asked myself why I think that I suck at writing and where that belief came from. The truth is, I really don't know where that came from or why I held on to this belief for so long. When I think about it, I've only had success at writing.

While I've never written a book before, I've written countless emails, business procedures, blog posts for a successful business, and website copy that lured in Fortune 500 companies as clients. I've even written rules to a board game that was eventually licensed by Arby's for a kids' meal program. So it was darned time that I threw away that limiting belief for good! And I think it's time that we all challenge and discard our self-limiting beliefs.

Limiting Ourselves

Limiting beliefs hold us back from being the best version of ourselves. They keep us stuck in patterns that don't serve us well.

I wasn't even aware of the term "limiting beliefs" until I signed up for relationship coaching after my last breakup. (Now I wish I had known about those coaches long ago!) My coach had me recount a typical situation where I continuously got hurt and upset with my boyfriend. So I talked about how, during times when he'd be really busy and distracted for what would seem to me like a long period of time, I would feel like I was being treated like chopped liver.

My coach asked me what I felt when my boyfriend would get distracted for these extended periods of time. I said I felt unvalued and unloved. He would be with me but not present and not really engaged with me and what was going on in my life. He wouldn't call me any of the sweet pet names like usual and would basically be pretty self-absorbed. He was relying a lot on me for emotional support during these times. But I wasn't getting back what I needed from him.

After this went on for many days, I would then start to feel distant and start to pull myself away from him. I'd then feel resentful toward him, and negative thinking about him would take up a lot of my time and attention. By the time I confronted him, I would be pretty drained, and nothing he could say at that moment would help. So even after he'd try to make up for it, I'd still not be satisfied. Eventually it would lead to a bigger, more destructive blow up.

Of course, he was never intentionally or consciously trying to do anything to me. But what I did learn through my coach was that Dave was triggering some trauma from my childhood, which would then unconsciously trigger long-standing, limiting beliefs that I had that I was not ever aware even existed.

My limiting belief was that my relationships would always end up with abandonment and loneliness. So naturally, I would interpret my boyfriend's withdrawal and silence as him not caring, and thus his lack of emotion became evidence (in my mind) that he was abandoning me. Of course, his withdrawal had nothing to do with me. He would just do this when he was overwhelmed with his own emotions from whatever stress he was dealing with. And then he would interpret my reaction as being clingy or insecure.

"Insecure" is not how anyone I know would label me. In fact, others in my life say they see me as a very secure and self-assured person, which is also how I see myself. However, when I'm triggered in the way described above, these limiting beliefs of feeling abandoned and uncared for would cause a lot of problems in our relationship.

Recognizing Limiting Beliefs

The way to fix any limiting belief is to first learn how to recognize it when it appears, examining how you're feeling in that moment, then replacing that old limiting belief with a more empowering belief. For me, that often meant shifting my thinking from "I'm being abandoned" to "My partner loves me and is just going through his own emotional battles, and it's not personal to me."

Another limiting belief that my coach helped me uncover was "I am responsible for everything," which would be triggered when I was feeling helpless about someone else's pain. This stemmed from childhood when I felt helpless when my younger siblings were being spanked with a two-by-four piece of wood and I could hear their cries of pain. I remember hiding under my bed crying, feeling so helpless. I was the oldest child and always felt responsible for my four younger siblings.

This limiting belief of "I am responsible for everything" would set in motion a pattern where I would self-sacrifice until I was depleted. Then by the time I eventually "checked out," my partner couldn't meet my needs. I would then disconnect with myself and my partner, which would then activate my flight mode with another limiting belief of "I am on my own essentially—this is the same thing all over again."

> I remember hiding under my bed crying, feeling so helpless. I was the oldest child and always felt responsible for my four younger siblings.

To change these limiting beliefs, I had to incorporate a new belief to replace that with "I am not responsible for everything, and that's okay." I had to look for facts in my life to support this new belief, such as recognizing friendships that are equal and balanced.

It's not that easy the first time you challenge those patterned conditions that form your limiting beliefs. At first, you'll have to battle that fear that comes up, that scary feeling that burns in your solar plexus. But once you start to make positive change happen yourself, and you see the positive results, you end up reprogramming yourself naturally. The positive rewards will burn new beliefs into your wiring.

Identifying your own limiting beliefs is an area where working with a life coach, business coach, or relationship coach can be incredibly eye opening and life changing. I cover more on this topic on my social media pages and invite you to connect with me (@jennabanks.0) on Instagram, Facebook, or TikTok.

How Have You Held Yourself Back?

Write down three things that you've been wanting to do for at least several years now, but that you haven't been able to do.

- Under each of these three items, list the resources you would need to accomplish these things.
- Now write why you haven't been able to accomplish each of these three goals. Write down at least two reasons for each goal.
- Take a look at the contrast between the resources you would need to accomplish each goal and the reasons why you believe you couldn't get these goals accomplished.
- Ask yourself if the contrast is reasonable or not. If you find that you wrote down any reasons that weren't based in reality or fact, then these are your limiting beliefs.
- Ask yourself why you believe that limiting belief, and write it down.
- Take a look at what you wrote, and ask yourself if it is a fact or a belief.
- If it's not a fact but a belief, try to figure out why you believe it to be true.

What we're trying to uncover are any stories or beliefs that you've been telling yourself that may have been preprogrammed because of experiences you've had prior to this one.

For example, let's take a look at my writing this book. If I had let the idea sit around in my head for years, and the reason I let it sit was because I believed "I suck at writing," well, that's not a fact. It's a belief that I've told myself forever. And if I were not aware of what limiting beliefs were, as I am now, I might have let that longstanding belief hold me back from starting to write. Once I was able to take a look at this belief when it popped up, I was able to see it for what it was and question it, rather than let it stop me from moving forward with my dreams and goals.

PART III

How to Put Yourself First

When you put yourself first, you are also teaching others how to treat you, and a more positive relationship cycle—with yourself and others—ensues. When you treat yourself with respect and honor, and don't feel beneath anyone or above anyone, you'll be treated with respect and honor by those around you, even admired by a coffee-craving company president (story to come). The secret to putting yourself first is that it does not require complex situations or complicated conversations. The opportunities for self-priority are found everywhere in the small stuff.

If you've ever walked out of the way of people on the street instead of ever making them make way for you; if you know what it's like to miss your favorite morning spin class to help a friend with her resume when it could wait until a time that would better work for you; if you have ever said yes to assisting with a project you have no interest in; if you keep turning the other cheek on constant last-minute plan changes (as if your time is not precious!), then you need help in learning how to put yourself first.

The good news is that there are subtle but powerful ways you can put yourself first. The things you can do to exude more control over how much you give, when you give, and why you give do not have to be so earth-shaking that they are cause for a parade. You don't need to shout from the rooftops that you're putting yourself first.

Instead, we can screw on a pair of self-priority training wheels. We can go slowly and make private decisions quietly. We can cherry-pick where we begin, gauge how far we are comfortable going, and practice over time.

Soon these personal decisions become solidified into a loving contract we make with ourselves: testing along the way, checking in with ourselves—and then more trial and more error—until we see that self-priority gets us further with others and ourselves than when we self-sacrifice.

The following chapters are chock full of ideas for how you can begin to take back your time, energy, and spirit, and stop putting your needs—large and small—at the back of the line. Here, you'll learn about the power of saying no to others and yes to yourself so you can take control of your time and attention (Chapter 12); how to avoid the trap of over-giving (Chapter 13); developing the strength to remove toxic relationships from your life (Chapter 14); what kinds of boundaries you should set for yourself (Chapter 15); and the freedom that comes from owning your whole story, not just the pretty bits (Chapter 16).

Together, these tactics create a solid foundation for putting yourself first and embracing your value and power.

Chapter 12

Taking Control of Your Time and Attention

had only been working as a business development manager at a technology consulting firm for a month or two. Still the new kid on the block, I was excited to meet the president, who had flown into town from India to spend the week visiting our office. My first time getting to meet him was during our Monday morning weekly company meeting. The president sat at the head of the table in the board room, turned toward me, and said as if in a private conversation, "It would be nice to have some coffee from the Starbucks downstairs. Would you like some coffee as well, Jenna?"

I actually didn't want coffee, so I responded, "No, thank you; I don't drink coffee this late in the day."

My boss, the company VP, just stared at me, his mouth gaping like I had just told this man to jump off a cliff or something. I could tell something was wrong but was out of the loop on whatever it was. Another colleague of mine, Mike, who had the same title as I did, tried to ease the tension in the room by rephrasing the question to me in the form of a not-so-subtle hint with eyebrow raises, something along the lines of, "Jenna, you love a good Starbucks latte, wouldn't you *love* a cup like right now?"

"No, Mike," I answered. "If I have coffee now, I'll be awake all night. I'll skip it."

The meeting went on, and we all survived without coffee. Afterward, when back at our desks, Mike asked me to help him learn to use the coffeemaker in the break room. "I don't know why you're asking me," I joked with Mike. "I've never used this darn thing."

I went about the rest of my day without giving this coffee conundrum a second thought. I didn't want or need coffee, so anyone who had the need for coffee had nothing to do with me. At the end of the day, when I popped my head into my boss's office to say good night, the company president was sitting across from my boss's desk. "Jenna," the president said, craning his neck from the chair, "I look up to you."

I had no idea where his compliment was coming from, so I jokingly said, "That's probably because I'm wearing heels." We all shared a laugh.

At home, I thought about the day and meeting the president and the situation about the coffee, which is when I realized the dynamic at play. Those guys fully expected me to get them coffee because *they* wanted coffee. They were so used to having their needs met, presumably by the women in their lives, that they didn't know how to react when their needs didn't trump my own. And it gained me respect! Why? Because my actions showed the company president that I regarded myself higher than him—not in a dog-eat-dog way and not in a rude or conceited, narcissistic way—but in a way that reminded him that we are all responsible for ourselves, and it is our own duty to fulfill our own needs. Even when you're the top dog.

This is a story I still like to tell even though it happened many years ago, because it is one of the simplest instances of the power of prioritizing yourself. Small gesture, big impact. There wasn't anything empirically selfish about not making coffee, it was just not top of mind to stop what I was doing to fetch something I had no desire for. Put another way, if I had a craving for coffee and announced to the group,

"I am dying for some Starbucks; I'm making a run, does anyone want anything?" then I'd be showing good manners. But making a Starbucks run for someone else's craving when I know I'm not buying myself any—well, that's just running errands, and last I checked, errand girl was not part of my job description.

Self-Sacrifice Is Not Always a Virtue

Putting others first, or self-sacrificing, is seen in many cultures as a virtue. Except I've never met a yes-person who is happy, fulfilled, or truly respected. While helping others can make us feel really good, we need to make sure that doing for others all the time isn't an act to placate our egos or to make us feel needed or important. I could've easily made coffee for the company president to earn brownie points, except I ultimately would've just shown him I'm a pushover, that I don't value myself, and lost points with him. Who wants a pushover in charge of sales?

Remember, placing so much emphasis on gaining external validation or "object-referral" is self-love sabotage. We need to understand that we are enough, whether we decide to constantly carpool half the Little League team, lend money to a friend in need, get coffee for the team—or not. Being raised a Christian, I do not say this lightly.

While I am not religious, but consider myself deeply spiritual, I was brought up reading the Bible often, going to church multiple times a week, and attending Christian schools. I was taught by my parents to try to live like Jesus did. In Christianity, we are taught about sacrifice: God sacrificed his only son for us, and Jesus gave the ultimate sacrifice—his life for our sins. In my house, this translated to "Self-sacrificing is a virtue." My stepmother commanded my siblings and me to give up things we wanted for ourselves, offering them to others, to each other, or even to complete strangers. Raised by a narcissistic father who didn't make it a priority to tend to the needs of his wife or children, I constantly gave in to whatever would make my father happy in order to keep the peace. In sacrificing ourselves and our needs, we become more like Jesus. Mother Teresa famously said, "Give until it hurts." And in many cases for me, it did.

This old programming of self-sacrifice has indeed hurt, especially because it has trickled into my romantic relationships. When I didn't put my own needs first and focused too much on my partner's needs, I became resentful when my needs weren't being met in return. However, the truth is that when I don't tend to my own needs, it's nobody else's fault. No one is responsible for meeting my needs; I am not responsible for meeting theirs. In the words of Roy T. Bennett, "Take responsibility of your own happiness, never put it in other people's hands."[1]

I get it. It feels completely counterintuitive to put yourself first. And frankly, I understand how hearing people say over and over again to "put yourself first," without any advice on how to actually accomplish this feat, can feel like an overplayed song on the radio—you just turn it off. You just don't want to hear it anymore.

Say Yes to Yourself

I recently stumbled across an article written for *NBC News* by a self-proclaimed compulsive giver, Laura Delarato. She had developed a bad habit of saying yes to others, which translated into a big fat no to her overall wellness.

So she committed herself to a thirty-day challenge, doing nothing but saying yes to *herself* for an entire month. To help the challenge stick, Laura categorized what she believed she personally needed to work on to put herself first in her world. The areas she identified as requiring "much-needed attention" were friendships, wellness, and dating. She didn't go overboard to address these issues, like ending life-long friendships or quitting a job. Rather, she looked for small changes when it came to navigating her three areas. For example, she stopped saying yes to social activities she had no desire to do, like going to crowded clubs and drinking (which, as a self-described homebody, she found intolerable). When it came to her wellness, she chose to spend her limited free time on weekends to do healthy meal prep and catch up on exercise in lieu of doing extra work or helping a friend. And my favorite: dating. Laura no longer twisted around her life for people she didn't know or care about, which she describes as "not traveling above 14th Street on a work night." Laura continues, "How many times have I gone to meet someone super far from my apartment to find out they're actually a horrible human? Too many."[2] I really admire Laura for taking this approach.

And what was the outcome of her thirty-day experiment? "This month-long journey, at times, felt like a me-only navigation through life; making decisions based on how I (and only I) felt," she writes. "I honestly thought by the end of it I'd have zero friends and nil prospects for dating. [But the reality was] quite the opposite in fact. Every friendship is stronger; giving each person my everything when I'm with them. Dating, while occurring less often, is happening with people who are 100 percent more attuned to our mutual interests. I make good decisions based off what I need in the moment."[3]

One of the ways I converted Laura's idea into action is to make a conscious effort to track how often I say yes to myself and not another person—I aim for one specific way, every day. This inspires me to identify areas where I might expend too much of myself when I don't want to, without becoming overwhelmed by engaging in a so-called complete life transformation. Don't get me wrong: I am very happy to give to others and to help when I've got the time and energy. But now I just make sure it's not at the expense of my own needs at the time.

Investing in Yourself

I have a friend, Michele, whose husband, while taking a close look at their finances, wanted her to quit her passion for Pilates. Apparently the Pilates studio is costly, and she pays a monthly membership that is equal to their steep cable bill. But Michele goes every single day, accomplishing the rare feat of working out every day. "I told my husband to stop looking at my daily practice as an expense and see it as an investment," Michele told me. "It is my 'me time,' yes, but it is also toning, stretching, core work, deep breathing, and meditation—all things any medical doctor would tell you to do for health and longevity. I'd rather spend a couple of hundred dollars a month to age well, avoid injury because I'm limber, and feel less resentful of the family duties because I know each day there is an hour with my name, and only my name, on it. And I actually go to the studio. Is it better to spend ten dollars a month on a gym membership you don't use at all or spend more money on a studio you practically live at?"

Michele's attitude is spot on. She believes her focus on her daily practice will be less costly in the long run than prescription co-pays, doctor visits for aches and pains, and paying to see a therapist for stress or anxiety. She is investing in her health—physical, mental, and emotional. Not only did her husband see the light; he joined Pilates with her! Now it's something that nurtures their relationship too.

If we spend our whole lives being reactive instead of proactive interest-takers in our own lives, we miss opportunities to expand and grow. Investing in yourself means that you believe in yourself. Invest in your interests and hobbies, invest in your love of travel, invest in you; you will reap major rewards—and so will others around you.

Entitlement versus Self-Priority

I want to be clear that putting yourself first implies that there is a threat you might be put second or third. This is an important distinction to remember when deciding what is an act of self-priority and what is just being a jerk. Keeping the wrong change the cashier gave you because it's free money, not holding the door for the old lady coming out of the building behind you because you have a train to catch, or cutting the line because you are late for a dentist appointment are not admirable "I matter" attitudes. They are indecent, entitled acts and have nothing to do with putting your needs first.

Your goal is to admire yourself. Admire the good choices you consciously make, the effort you put into your work, the good friend that you are, the hard work you put in to get something you really wanted. Admire yourself when you stand up for yourself and your convictions or when you choose to walk away from a relationship that isn't serving you well. Strive to make yourself proud, because your opinion of yourself is the only opinion that really matters. Love who you are and what you stand for. You'll find a love so much deeper than any you've ever known before.

An Investment with High Return

When you invest in a stock, bet on a horse, or put your money aside to send a child to college, you are saying you believe in that stock, horse, or child, and you expect a return on your investment.

I've never second-guessed spending money to educate myself or follow my entrepreneurial inspirations. I also never hesitate to take time between jobs to recharge, focus on spiritual growth, and recalibrate goals. Yes, I might have to go through some of my savings to do that, but that's an investment in me, and I'm worth it. If I show myself that I'm willing to invest in myself, my sense of self-worth and self-confidence increases exponentially. And when you feel self-confident, the world will take notice of your self-confident energy and will in turn feel confident in you as well.

I'm urging you to do the same for yourself. When you stop saying yes to others all the time and instead place the highest priority on your own needs, that is making an investment in yourself. And it's an investment that pays great dividends.

What Are Some of the Ways in Which You Could Invest in Yourself and Build Your Sense of Self-Worth?

Write down in your journal some ways in which you would feel good about investing in yourself now or in the near future. Would you like to get a special certification, hire a personal trainer, get some professional photographs, get a new wardrobe, take an online course? There are so many ways in which we can put our own money back into ourselves to show ourselves that we are worth our own investment.

Chapter 13

Avoid the Trap of Over-giving

Have you heard the story about the woman who played wife, mother, nursemaid, career woman, PTA president, soccer coach, and caretaker to her aging parents for pretty much her whole damn life? Over time she gained a ton of weight, rarely laughed, and had very little money because she constantly "lent" it to others. If she did have a spare ten bucks, she felt obligated to toss it into the charity pot outside the supermarket during the holiday season. This woman planned birthday celebrations for all the members of her family, but on her birthdays made her own dinner and cleared the table! She even turned down a much-needed trip to Florida to meet her old college classmates because she felt obligated to help with a PTA fundraiser.

One day, soon after her last child went off to college, she'd noticed she'd aged terribly; let herself go, as they say. No wonder she and her husband no longer connected beyond him adding items to her grocery list. She had entered menopause feeling old, lonely, and utterly purposeless. Looking back, each duty she performed, each time she didn't express her disappointment for not receiving a birthday wish or thank you, each time she gave away her time, her talent, her energy, and her care to someone else in lieu of focusing it on herself—all this chipped, chipped, chipped away at her soul until there was nothing left.

I hate to be a Debbie Downer, but this story is not an exaggeration. It is what happens over time when you ignore something (someone) important. Ever see what happens to a house that is not maintained? A monument that is not cleaned or tended to? A sports car that isn't winterized? It's not good!

Are you over-giving like this woman did? To whom are you giving and what do you give? Learning the answer could take a lot of soul-searching and observation.

Over-giving Is Everywhere

The universality of over-giving became clear to me after reading the writings of Elizabeth Gilbert, famous for her best-selling memoir, *Eat, Pray, Love.* Gilbert wrote on Oprah.com that she has always been an over-giver, even as a child. But when she struck it rich, she became an over-giver of money.

She was doing as Mother Teresa said to do, giving until it hurts, and according to Elizabeth it did wind up hurting her. "My whole life I've been an over-giver," she wrote in her post "Confessions of an Over-Giver." "Over the years, I have over-given with my money, my stuff, my opinions, my time, my body ('I know we've only just met, but of course we can make out in your cousin's car!') . . . I am especially over-giving toward people I just met yesterday afternoon at the gas station."[1]

Boy, does this sound familiar. Especially the part about offering my opinions or advice. I am passionate about helping others, but I can really over-give my emotional support when asked by pretty much anybody, as if *their* emotional life is somehow *my* responsibility. In my life, over-giving emotional support has fatigued me, and quite frankly in some cases sucked the life out of me.

I can really over-give emotional support when asked by pretty much anybody, as if *their* emotional life is somehow *my* responsibility.

Encounter with an Energy Vampire

I had a decade-long friendship with a woman I will call Tina. I could best describe how she emotionally hijacked me as "razzle-dazzle." She razzle-dazzled me with her well-kept appearance, the good-looking people she surrounded herself with, the fun events and dinners at trendy restaurants she took me to. Tina introduced me to a lot of people (though that didn't really matter much to me, since my career and motherhood were my priorities and I didn't have time for more people in my life). Tina texted and called several times a day, and she was pretty much the main "friend" in my life for quite a few years (and I use those quote marks deliberately).

As we spent more time together, she started taking new, disrespectful liberties, like getting demanding with me or commenting on things I was doing; she put me down and criticized me. I began to feel like I was being treated like a beck-and-call girl to her. When she needed me for advice, none of which she ever took (so frustrating!), she'd expect me to stop whatever I was doing and listen to her stories. She wanted to dominate and control me, and she did so with her passive-aggressive nature. Backhanded compliments were really put-downs. She'd make me listen to the same dramatic "problems," which she never did anything about solving, and even picked on my own life choices, despite the fact that I had never asked her opinion.

In short, she was over-taking and expecting me to over-give. *Chip, chip, chip.*

Finally, I spoke to her about how I felt she was crossing boundaries and treating me poorly. I figured if we were such great friends, we could hold a candid conversation and move on from there. Well, that never happened. Tina apparently couldn't handle being challenged and got defensive and went into attack mode.

Afterward, Tina tried to bad-mouth me to mutual friends. She proceeded to try to get our mutual friends to turn on me, trying to get them to choose a side, as if we were in high school. I felt like an idiot to have let this kind of person control so much of my precious time and energy.

Thankfully, our mutual friends saw right through her and didn't let Tina influence their feelings toward me. She ended up doing me the biggest favor by eliminating herself from my life. I lost an energy vampire and gained life-long, true friends whom I adore and who truly love me. As Bernard Baruch is believed to have said, "Be who you are, and say what you feel, because those who mind don't matter, and those who matter don't mind." Since that experience, I learned never to let any one person in my life gain that much control over my attention and energy. Not a boyfriend, not a friend, not even my own son. (I've dedicated an entire chapter to boundary setting as parents, so stay tuned.)

Seven Signs You Are Over-giving

Knowing the signs of over-giving can really help, especially when you're trying to maintain the boundaries you are setting in your life. Putting yourself first is a lifelong practice, and we can certainly slip back into our old habits of giving away too much. It's catching our over-giving at the very first "chip" that is key to turning patterns around.

So how can you determine if you are over-giving? According to Kara Laricks, matchmaker and dating expert, "To determine if you are an over-giver, start by asking yourself, 'Am I an under-getter?' I often find that in relationships, over-giving, whether in time, availability, attention, sex, or gifts is a sure sign that *you* are not getting the time, attention, etc., that you desire in a relationship."[2]

It's important to pay attention to how you feel around people, situations, and conversations. Being empathetic is a great quality. But it's very easy for empathetic people to let their attention and energy get swept away by other people. According to *Bustle* magazine, there are seven ways to take note if you are giving away too much of yourself in your relationships.[3] Whether you use them as guidelines, red flags, or moments of clarity, noting any one of them can help you draw a line in the sand when it comes to over-giving in your relationship, whether it's with an intimate partner, friend, coworker, or boss.

1. *You don't know how to receive.* This can apply to receiving attention, compliments, gifts, or another person's generosity with their time, energy, or guidance. Basically, this is code for "you don't ask for help!" Looking back, I found that I didn't ask for help when I really could have used it, deflected most compliments, and didn't allow others to be there for me for fear of putting them out.

2. *Your partner's enthusiasm for all that you're doing is fading.* In my early days dating Dave, he was so generous with his gratitude for whatever it was I did for him, and over time, I felt my giving became a major expectation of our relationship.

3. *Your partner's needs always come first.* I basically did the drop-and-roll for Tina and Dave. I am glad I had these experiences, however, because now I know how I will not live in the future. I also recognize this as a red flag in a new friendship and relationship. If it's all about them, I'm out.

4. *You "like" everything your partner likes.* While I don't suffer from this issue, it's a great one to help you recognize whether you are losing parts of yourself in a relationship. We all know the friend who began only hanging around her boyfriend's friends or started changing her staunch political views to align with her husband's, or began taking shopping sprees with her new bestie, even though she hates malls. Don't chip away at your time, and don't allow other people to change you—another terrific sign of a red flag that might signal you to save yourself!

5. *You're emotionally spent.* I knew this was true of me based on my energy level. With Dave and Tina, I felt like I simply had run out of steam and had nothing left for anyone else, much less myself. I couldn't give one more ounce of myself and became lethargic,

suffered attention span issues, and had a low-grade malaise. Listen to your body; it's your signpost telling you when something is not right.

6. *You feel resentful.* I tried to channel my resentment into having a grown-up conversation with Tina. Even though I didn't get the outcome I expected, I am glad I could take my resentment and do something productive with it. Doing so helped me free up my energy and use it for more productive things, like taking care of me!

7. *You believe it's your responsibility to keep the relationship together.* Guilty. Well, at least half guilty. I didn't necessarily *believe* it was my responsibility to keep our relationship going, but I did bear the burden. I felt like I had to tend to the energy of our relationship to the point when I confronted Dave on the one-sided nature of our relationship, resulting in him tasking me with "helping him" to meet my needs. Which only meant I was still bearing the brunt of the responsibility of the relationship. It was time to go.

If you are constantly in reaction mode, you are not in control of your energy. Knowing your boundaries on how much you will give allows you to be in control of where your energy goes and to whom. It will also help you determine the quality of the people in your life and naturally eliminate those who are interested only in controlling you and your energy/attention and who don't have your best interest at heart. In the words of Iyanla Vanzant, "When you start sacrificing yourself for other people, you make them a thief, because they are stealing from you what you need, and they don't even know it."[4]

Giving, but Not Too Much

In previous chapters, I talk about how I over-gave in my relationship with Dave. I didn't see it at first, mistaking my giving for an act of loving him. He didn't ask for all the things I was doing for him. I was just conditioned to think that self-sacrificing was an act of love. When you are an over-giver, you are possibly seeking ways to justify the love you are trying to receive because you either believe you aren't worthy without doing all this giving, you fear abandonment, or perhaps you are modeling behavior from a parent or other family member.

We over-givers typically tend to know that we do it, so it's important to go a step further than acceptance and take stock of where we see ourselves giving too much away. Otherwise, we will wind up being taken advantage of and taken for granted, like the woman I described at the beginning of this chapter, and like I was in my relationship with Dave. I say this from experience, not from a psychological perspective.

It's okay to give yourself to others, but you have to be careful not to give too much of yourself away to anyone. It's important to your self-care and self-love to set clear boundaries for yourself. You need to love yourself more than anyone else and take full ownership of your energy. If you don't own it, others will.

Chapter 14

Detox from Toxic Relationships

cannot begin to tell you how freeing it's been for my spirit to have eliminated all the toxic relationships from my life. I have never once looked back and regretted any decision to cut ties with those who only brought me down. It is both fortunate and unfortunate that I've had to cut ties with people close to me, beginning at the age of fourteen, when I left home, and again at sixteen, when I left my mother's toxic house and never looked back.

Let me share some examples from my own life to illustrate how to recognize toxic relationships and how to detox yourself from them.

A BFF Who Wasn't

Choosing to break up with my one-time best friend, Wendy, with whom I spent a lot of time between the ages of sixteen and eighteen, revealed to me just how much of yourself can be taken away by a peer.

Once we left our teenage years behind us, both Wendy's and my lives changed. Wendy got married and had a couple of children. I also married, moved to the Netherlands, and had a son. Back then, without technology, with an ocean between us and the daily pressures of adulthood, we grew apart and didn't connect very regularly. But when we did, I always felt that she would find a way to make me feel bad or put me down. She was never positive about anything happening in my life. That, to me, is one definition of toxic.

After I moved back to the States and settled into my life in California, I received a call from Wendy, after going more than a year without talking. It was her tone, her probing questions that felt more like judgment, her reactions to whatever I was saying that made me feel like she was acting superior. You know when you get off the phone or after a visit with someone and you feel like you want to scrub the ick off yourself? Well, that's how I felt after we hung up.

But after that last phone call from Wendy, I thought to myself, *Why do I keep this person in my life? What kind of value does she add to my life? She doesn't make me a better person; she doesn't contribute anything, not even giving me a good feeling to take with me throughout the day. I don't feel good connecting with her anymore.* She was really just an old connection, not someone I'd consider a real friend. So I made the decision that I would stop all connection with her. This decision alone made me feel good, so I never questioned it.

A few months later, Wendy tried to get in touch again. I never responded, and she went away. Guess what? I never had that feeling of someone making me feel "less than" again. If I had let her remain in my life, I would have been allowing myself to be treated this way. I would've been putting that kind of energy into the world, and all I would've gotten in return is more negativity. Now, I could have also confronted her with my feelings, like I did with Tina, and given her the opportunity to change her approach with me, but my instinct told me we didn't have enough in common anymore to create a new dynamic.

My Second (and Final) Breakup with Dave

As I talk about in previous chapters, I'd never felt the kind of love for someone that I felt for Dave, which made it incredibly intoxicating. I fell for him hard, and for a long time I thought of him as a person I could spend the rest of my life with. I'd get a little bit of excitement even just from a call or text from him. You may recall that I broke up with Dave because he was not meeting my needs. But what I didn't reveal was that we actually got back together not too long after that dinner I had with Emily, mentioned at the beginning of this book.

My friend Emily and I bumped into Dave and one of his friends at that same restaurant where Emily and I had discussed my initial breakup. The four of us ended up talking with each other at the restaurant bar. After a while, we decided to go dancing. Emily and Dave's friend were doing their best to keep us together for as long as possible that evening. After many hours and quite a few drinks, it was hard not to feel the attraction and chemistry between us. While he was incredibly charming and flirtatious, I was the one who made the move on him, and it definitely wasn't thought out at all. But we ended up reconnecting that evening. The next day, with more sober heads about us, we decided it would be a good idea to get together and talk about things.

In my mind, there was no way that Dave would say anything to me that would convince me he had changed his ways. I remember telling a friend that the likelihood he'd come around and be able to meet my relationship needs was probably less than 5 percent. And still I met him for lunch to "talk." I showed up with no expectations whatsoever. I showed up in my full power and sense of self-worth. I showed up not needing anything from him, just fully present and alert to hearing what he had to say, but fully expecting it wouldn't be what I needed to hear.

To my complete surprise, quite the opposite happened. He addressed every concern I had and made it clear that he wanted a real relationship with me—even wanted to become life partners. I was beaming, so elated and so convinced that all our problems were now resolved and that we were ready to build a life together. (Ah, false hope.)

After around eight or nine months passed, things had been going so well between us that we decided to move in together. We figured it would either take our relationship to the next level or we'd somehow crash and burn.

We found a really cool house to rent close to where we were both already living and were super excited for this fun new adventure together. I made sure to address what I thought were some important things for us to keep in mind while living together, such as not going to bed angry and prioritizing clear and open communication to keep our relationship healthy. These were some of my relationship values. He agreed with these things, so I thought surely we were prepared to go into this new living situation fully equipped with the right mindset to get us through anything.

Just a couple of weeks after we moved in, I already felt pretty unhappy. I had been doing a lot to help Dave out with his life, house, and business, and wasn't feeling valued or appreciated. The whole "chopped liver" feeling kept coming up for me again, but now I was feeling it more often. The toxicity had returned. I also just didn't feel like my normal, happy, balanced self. My power container was once again being depleted.

To top things off, our sex life fizzled after the first week. I kept trying to fix things by self-sacrificing. But it was really hard for me to focus on building my new business, since I just wasn't feeling like myself. Well, you know what happened after that. I went round two with a broken heart over someone I was ready to spend the rest of my life with (twice). Why did I go back? Why—knowing there was a miniscule chance he would be able to be someone he wasn't or give what he isn't capable of giving—did I ignore my intuition?

We Love the Familiar (Even If It's Toxic)

Have you ever heard that old saying about people falling for partners who remind them of one of their parents? I never thought that would happen to me, since my father and I didn't have any relationship at all after I left home. It's hard to feel love toward someone, or bond with them, when you fear them as a dominator who squelches your spirit and doesn't show love for you unconditionally.

I also didn't care for my father. I didn't hate him or anything. I just didn't think he should have had kids, and I didn't respect him for how he chose to parent. And yet, come to find out, as humans we have some sort of vulnerability in our operating systems. We tend to fall hard for people who have patterns that are familiar to us, despite the fact that there may be a ton of red flags about that person and they might not meet our core relationship values and desires.

There's something comforting when we feel a familiar pattern with someone. It feels instantly safe because it's a known feeling. If you had a good relationship with your father, and then find yourself in relationships with men who remind you of your father, I guess that wouldn't be a bad thing. However, it is still good to be aware that it is our natural tendency to feel comfortable around people with familiar patterns.

Did you know that if you are still feeling butterflies in your stomach when you're around the person you're dating, or when they call you or text you, that it's actually probably not a good thing? According to relationship expert Talia Goldstein, "People feel like butterflies are a good thing, but if you still have butterflies [after a few dates], I think that's not a good thing." Goldstein continues, "Sometimes it means that there's anxiety or that you're unsure of a situation. A good match is somebody that makes you feel calm and comfortable."[1]

I can bear witness to this, as Dave and I had a very exciting and fun relationship. But, during our relationship, I would also experience general feelings of anxiety, which was not something that was normal for me. I'd also get butterflies every time he'd call or text me— also not something I was used to. I thought I was just excited to hear from him. Come to find out, these "butterflies" were a sign of stress and anxiety.

Love and sex release dopamine in the brain, a chemical involved in reward and motivation. It's interesting to me to think about drug addicts who get addicted to a particular drug and continue to use it, even if it's harming them. They are just addicted to getting that feeling, that chemical release in the brain that feels so good when it's there. But when it's gone, the addict misses that feeling terribly and will go out and use again just to feel that good feeling again, despite the negative consequences. We can look at that situation and know that it's not good for the drug user.

When people we love are using drugs, it's easy to sit back and say, "Get off the drugs, get into rehab. The dopamine release you are feeling when you use drugs is having negative consequences in your life." Yet no one warns us in life of the highly addictive nature of sex and love. Once we get hooked and get used to that feeling, that dopamine release (yep, the same chemicals get released in our brain whether it's sex, love, or drugs), our rose-colored glasses go on and we tend to overlook all the red flags. We forget about ourselves, forgetting to ensure that before we jump into full-fledged drug addiction, we first determine whether this person is actually capable of meeting our needs or has the values we are looking for.

Once we are hooked, all the other stuff, the most important stuff, seems to go out the window. Thus, we end up addicted to love, until it wears off, and we then go back to being able to see the person for who they really are.

Now I can look back and see so many red flags that should have warned me not to go down the path I went down with Dave. So many boundaries I let us both cross. So many indications that he was truly not capable of being the partner that I would need to truly thrive in a relationship.

I take full responsibility for my part in this becoming a toxic relationship. But at least I was able to identify it and save myself from being fully consumed by it. We've only got one life to live. Why live it in a toxic relationship of any kind?

Detox Can Be Painful

After my last relationship with Dave ended, I swear I felt like I was going through major withdrawals. Even though I'd made a conscious, instinctual decision to leave that relationship, my body craved that love drug so badly. My heart felt like there was a huge hole in it. My mind kept played tricks on me, making me think I could somehow accept things as they were and go back. I was detoxing just as I would have from any other drug.

But the truth was, I wasn't being shown real love by Dave, at least not the type of love I would need to be in a committed relationship with someone I planned to make a future with. I had to see the reality of what he was showing me, and telling me, during the few post-breakup calls that we had—that this lack of love was the truth. He showed no emotion whatsoever about the breakup. He was nice to me, honestly. It seemed like he might have been fishing, fishing to see he still had my heartstrings to play with. But he gave me no kind of indication that he had any lingering feelings toward me or that he missed me or really cared about me at all. I had to tell myself that my body was just craving that dopamine release that I had from being "in love" and from giving him so much love. But the love wasn't even real. It was just my addiction to the chemical release. Once I pulled away, the truth of what was really there was difficult to deny. I couldn't unsee what I observed or unfeel what I now felt.

At the time, I decided to gain as much knowledge about myself and the relationship and learn as much as I could from it. I didn't want my emotions to control me; I wanted to understand them fully, as well as understand what really happened in this relationship. I started journaling

I didn't want my emotions to control me; I wanted to understand them fully as well as understand what really happened in this relationship.

every day, researched as much as I could online, got a relationship coach, read books, and reread books like *Attached* and *The Power of Now*. It took a good month or so of a lot of soul-searching, introspection, and allowing my feelings and emotions to work their way through me. But on the other side, I got my peace back. I got my power back. I got *me* back.

Getting over Dave was a hard-fought battle that took me months to fully get through. But damn if I didn't feel back to my joyous, productive self after several weeks. Side note: I did have to block all contact with him for quite a while, because contact with him would put my progress into a tailspin. But I kept putting my needs first. And it paid off! All that anxiety, stress, and negative mental energy was gone. My soul felt the elation that it had become so accustomed to feeling before I got into that toxic situation. I absolutely did the right thing for myself, and I pat myself on the back for fighting so hard and for winning that battle for myself.

Still, no matter how logical I could be about it, there was a ton of pain to deal with, for months after the breakup. That's just the nature of how addiction works. Eventually the pain from the withdrawal did subside. But I have to tell you that, even now, the thought of Dave brings a bit of excitement. Like the kind you would get from the thought of doing a drug that you might have once had fun with but quit doing because you know it wasn't beneficial to your life.

Just like doing drugs, dopamine withdrawal can make your brain play all kinds of tricks on you to try to get you to "feel better" by getting the drug again. Thankfully I'm a strong person and I stayed true to myself and what I wanted in life. On paper, Dave was none of the things I wanted or needed in a relationship. Doing that "relationship needs" assessment really helped me see clearly, in black and white, that he never shared my relationship values. (I discuss relationship values much more in Part VI.)

What he did provide me with was a lot of excitement, anxiety, and familiarity. Yet he was not even close to being good for me. I was an addict, willing to do all kinds of things to support this drug addiction, to my own sacrifice and detriment, taking away from my individual goals, and putting so much of myself and my resources into him instead of into myself where it belonged.

Cutting Ties with My Father

As you may recall from previous chapters, I stood up to my father when I was fourteen. Afterward, he basically didn't have much of anything to do with me. After I went to live with my mother, he and I had almost no contact.

As I grew up and became a normal, functioning adult, a mother, and an entrepreneur, my father got into the routine of calling me once a year to say hello, like he does now with his four other children. His calls would always make me emotional, recalling my childhood, the judgment stemming from his political and religious beliefs, and an overall sense of feeling small, like I could never be myself with him, like I was never accepted for who I was.

One day, he decided he'd call me on my birthday, something he never did, and called from a blocked number. When I answered the phone, I was unpleasantly surprised and instantly deflated. All those negative feelings came up for me, as they always did when he called. I felt like that little girl, not able to say anything to protect myself.

After we hung up, I was so sad and in such a terrible mood. Then this great courage inside of me came leaping out of my chest. My inner warrior goddess was like, *Enough is enough. I need to put my foot down. This is my life, and I will not let anyone bring me down like this.* So I went with that feeling and didn't second-guess it. I felt as though I'd rather jump into the fire and make a massive change than accept this negative energy in my life.

I had no idea what I'd say or what I wanted as the outcome, but I immediately picked up my phone and dialed his number. When he answered, I told him how dare he call me from a blocked number so that I'd be ambushed. I also told him that he ruined my birthday and asked him how he could live with himself doing that to me when there is no way on earth that he could think from the tone of my voice during that phone call that I was happy that he'd called or that I was enjoying the conversation. And in typical fashion, he flatly said, "Don't worry, I'll never call you again." And he never did.

I'm so happy that I stood up for myself; doing so actually salvaged the rest of my birthday because it felt exhilarating and liberating to have been me, my authentic self.

A Lightness of Being

Obviously, any relationship in which you are not saying yes to yourself or over-giving is a toxic one. In fact, the majority of people I know are well aware of who the toxic people are their lives. Dr. Stan Kapuchinski calls the people in our lives who make us miserable "PDIs," or "Personality Disordered Individuals." According to Dr. Kapuchinski, we all have a PDI in our life, and we allow them to stick around, no matter how toxic they are.

In his book *Say Goodbye to Your PDI*, Dr. Kapuchinski warns, "PDIs have expectations like 'Never criticize me,' 'Always be there,' 'Give me all of your attention,' 'Take all my hurt away,' 'Don't get close,' 'You are here to serve only me,' and 'Always treat me as extra special.'"[2] Kapuchinski stresses that we will never be able to please a PDI, so stop the insanity!

As I learned from my relationships with Wendy, Dave, and my father, what connected us was a shared history. I think history is a huge factor for why so many people put up with their PDIs. It was as if, because we had this history together, I felt compelled, even obligated, to keep the connection.

After each of these breakups with toxic people, however, I felt lighter, happier, and more joyous. In hindsight, I can see how much those toxic relationships had been weighing me down energetically. I don't know if I would have ever gone on to accomplish as much as I've been able to if that energy was still creating so much toxicity in my life. I no longer have any room for toxic relationships. I've learned how joyous my life is when I'm free of them. There's no going back!

JOURNALING SUGGESTION

Detoxing

- Reflect on and write down any relationships that you currently have in your life that bring you down rather than lift you up.
- Why do you keep them in your life?
- What would happen if you decided to stop communicating with these people? Would you miss them? Would your life be better or worse if they weren't in your life?

Chapter 15

Who's Afraid of the Big Bad Boundary?

People with poor boundary skills are susceptible to
peer pressure and easily cowed.

—Henry Cloud and John Townsend, *Boundaries*

Really, what have we been talking about in the previous chapters? Saying no, not chipping away at your soul, putting yourself first, avoiding toxic relationships—these are all acts of boundary setting. Are you shivering just thinking about putting up some walls or electric fences around what you consider your greatest priority—you? When it comes to setting boundaries, we are afraid. Doing so might make us look callous, unkind, selfish.

Dr. Henry Cloud and Dr. John Townsend literally wrote the book on boundaries, *Boundaries: When to Say Yes, How to Say No to Take Control of Your Life*. The book has sold over four million copies, so it's safe to say we are not alone in our need for help in boundary setting.

The authors ask us to think about boundaries in the physical sense.[1] The physical environment is defined by concrete boundaries, and there are several reasonable explanations for these boundaries. For instance, a barbed wire fence might encase a nuclear power plant to protect people from entering dangerous areas.

Boundaries are just as important for emotional and spiritual protection. Though perhaps not as clear-cut as physical boundaries, emotional boundaries are just as necessary. I love setting up the context of physical boundaries because it helps show that boundaries are logical and not arbitrary—that when we set our own emotional boundaries, we are being territorial over our well-being and helping others see where their boundaries lie, which is typically on the other side of "the fence." Just like giving someone their personal space is a "thing," so should giving them emotional space. Boundaries are designed for purposes of safety and well-being, so we should feel less afraid of the big, bad boundary—grateful, in fact.

According to Cloud and Townsend, it's difficult to establish your boundaries or discern other people's because it isn't always obvious when you should enforce them. But enforcing your boundaries shouldn't make you feel mean; in fact, it will help you feel better about yourself in the long run. Setting boundaries is an act of kindness.[2] And according to Iyanla Vanzant, it's an act of kindness toward God: "You put yourself last. How you treat yourself is how you treat God. So you're putting God last, because you are the representative of God in your life."[3]

What Boundaries Look Like

When most people think about "boundary setting," they think about physical boundaries, as in who is allowed to touch you and in what ways. But there many other types of boundaries that people can establish. I've found inspiration from Cloud and Townsend's book. The authors push us to think outside the box in terms of what boundaries we want to set for ourselves. Here are some of the more unusual items from their list of areas where we should consider setting boundaries:

- Words: for example, what we say yes to and what we say no to
- Truth: being honest about who you are and what you want

- Time: making conscious decisions to devote your time to yourself and people who value and respect you
- Emotional distance: taking space when you need it to get a clear head
- Consequences: making sure people know how serious you are about protecting yourself and respecting yourself
- Feelings: being aware of your true feelings and taking responsibility for them
- Resources and gifts: how and when you share (and don't share) your money, talents, and gifts
- Thoughts: setting boundaries on your thoughts and not letting them run wild[4]

To learn about other boundaries we might want to set, check out Cloud and Townsend's book.

Learning to Establish Boundaries

As a bred people pleaser, I don't particularly like confrontation; the thought of making others uncomfortable creates anxiety and discomfort within me. Mulling over these examples of boundaries prompted me to consider when I began exercising my boundaries, aside from refusing to live under my father's rules and leaving home at a young age. When was my first conscious act of defending my boundary?

To explain how it came about, I need to provide some background. During the couple of years that I lived with my mother, she left me horrible, psychologically abusive letters to come home to. Her blows were intentionally meant to crush my soul. And she succeeded. I was an incredibly sensitive child who had just come from a very sheltered Christian environment. I had been thrown into a home that was the complete opposite of how I'd been raised. I cried myself to sleep so many nights that eventually I became numb. Her abusive letters were very emotionally scarring for me.

After bouncing around from neighbors' houses to friends' places, at the age of seventeen I went to live with my maternal grandparents for what turned out to be not quite a full year. I was my grandmother's first grandchild, and as I've written, she was the first and only person to show me what it's like to have someone show you unconditional love. Without her, I'd never have known what that was like. I consider myself extremely lucky to have had both her and my grandfather in my life.

After I'd lived with my grandparents for just around a month or so, the three of us were sitting down for dinner. My grandmother was nagging me (at least that's what a teenager would think) about something, and I snapped at her, raising my voice to her and telling her to stop.

The next day I received a typed letter from my grandfather basically telling me that I had been extremely rude to my grandmother, that he wouldn't stand for it, and I could just leave as far as he was concerned. The letter hit me hard, triggering the trauma I'd developed having been the recipient of my mother's abusive letters. My one safe place suddenly didn't feel stable, and I badly needed some stability in my life. And I really needed to feel safe with my grandfather.

I read that letter over and over and realized that beneath the words was someone who was hurt and upset by my actions. My grandfather was expressing a boundary he set, which was that he and my grandmother were to be respectfully spoken to. I also realized he probably didn't have any clue the trauma that I'd been through with my mother, especially my history with her nasty letters.

So I mustered up the exact same courage that I'd found within myself when I confronted my father and decided to change the course of the outcome of my grandfather's letter, as well as my reaction to it. I decided to speak up about my own boundaries.

My heart was racing. I had to fight against all the thoughts within my head telling me that I should just play it safe and not rock the boat. I knew that there was no going back after I said my piece. I rehearsed what I had to say to him well enough in my head before confronting him so I could be sure I covered all the important issues, rather than having an emotional outburst.

I walked into my grandfather's office and asked if we could talk for a minute, letter in hand. I started off letting him know that I was very sorry that I upset him when I raised my voice at my grandmother and that it wouldn't happen again. Then I asked him to do me a favor: "If you ever have any issues with me in the future, could you please bring it up to me in person?" I explained how hurtful it was for me to get such a harsh letter from the person I loved and that I had been shell-shocked from previous letters from my mother.

Right away my grandfather thanked me for coming to him to talk to him about my feelings and promised he'd never write me any letters like that again. He also apologized for hurting me and for being so harsh. His response encouraged a life-long determination within me to become aware of my big boundaries and express them in a manner that would be empathetic and calm (not reactive) so that it would create lasting change within a relationship. In doing so, I created a more loving relationship with myself.

Creating Boundaries in Our Professional Lives

By way of preview for Part IV, putting ourselves first and setting boundaries can also have a profound impact on how we get ahead in the business world. Knowing my value and setting boundaries that support it has enabled me to turn my GED into a lifetime of career success, unrelenting grit, entrepreneurial acumen, and financial freedom. The next chapter takes a deep dive into the importance of knowing your value, in particular why it is critical and often overlooked when it comes to the practice of loving yourself more.

Monitoring Your Boundaries

I find that knowing when my boundaries are being crossed as well as how to stand up for them is difficult even when I know what I *want* to have happen. I suspect it is this area that many people struggle with.

One technique I use to help me become more aware of my boundaries and learn how to enforce them better is to reflect on any boundary-crossing situations I encounter. When I reflect back and feel like I didn't leave the situation feeling in my power but instead felt deflated, I try to figure out a better way to deal with a similar situation next time.

For example, recently I was at a restaurant with a friend, sitting at the bar, when a man that I know through shared acquaintances came to sit next to us. We also all knew a couple of other people at the establishment. We were all being very friendly, laughing and having a great time. Then he proceeded to slide his hand on my back, albeit very briefly, but in a way that was like a boyfriend would do, like he was trying to stake his claim to those around us. I wasn't flirting with him at all. But I was being friendly with him as was everyone else in our group.

After he did this a couple of times, I said, "Hey, boundaries, Bob. I'm not your girlfriend, so don't touch me like I am." But I said it nicely with a smile. He stopped for a minute. But then not too long after that, he did it again. My mind was working furiously wondering how to handle this. The man was not a stranger, and he knows people that I know, and I didn't want to make the situation more awkward. This man ended up leaving before I reached a point where I would have had to be more forceful with my words and actions.

The fact that I left that situation feeling a bit disempowered made me feel icky. And anytime I feel a bit icky after an encounter with someone, I reflect on it to try to understand it better. What I realized was that being nice with aggressive guys doesn't work. I should have firmly told him, "Don't touch me!" That would have sent a very clear message, especially to a boundary crosser like this guy was. Now, I humorously refer to any man who rather aggressively tests my boundaries as a "Boundaries Bob."

I knew that "icky" feeling from my experiences growing up. We kids were taught to believe that we could not set boundaries because they were allowed to be crossed by any adult in our lives whenever the adult wanted. So I had to learn how to pay attention to, and give energy to, exactly how I felt anytime I didn't feel good after an encounter with someone.

You Have a Right to Your Boundaries

Boundary setting has been, and probably still is, one of my biggest challenges. That's why, when I feel myself slipping and leaving my boundaries vulnerable, I remember that I have to make a conscious effort to be aware of my boundaries and defend them, just as any partner or loving parent would defend their loved one. Each time I successfully defend my boundaries, it feels quite empowering.

The more I've paid attention to boundaries, the more baffled I get by how they are constantly being tested in our daily lives. For example, one of my ex-boyfriends once sent me a message on social media, after twenty years of us not having any contact at all. At the time when he reached out, I was dating someone. So to ensure my reply was construed as platonic, I tossed in a mention of my new boyfriend. The ex and I exchanged a couple of benign messages that day—"You good?" "Yes, all is good." Okay great, we seemed to have closed that conversation loop.

When he first reached out, I hadn't really stopped to consider how I really felt about his attempt at reconnecting. But I didn't give it much thought again, since I felt the conversation loop had ended and that would probably be the end of it for another twenty years or more, as far as I was concerned.

But then, not too long after that interaction, he commented on one of my social media accounts just like any of my friends and family would do. When I saw his comment, what I felt in my body was like someone uninvited was intruding on my personal space. It was just a comment on a post, so I had the option to ignore it. But I had to be honest with myself about this feeling.

The old me would have not wanted to make him, or anyone else, feel bad. And so the old me would have just let it happen and wouldn't have done anything about it. But the me of today knows I have to protect my own boundaries, stand up for myself, and put myself first on my list of priorities.

This ex had crossed a boundary and so now I needed to protect my personal space. I sent him a note stating that we were not "friends" and never were. I reminded him that we had a relationship that ended because he violated my trust and had been quite dishonest with me throughout our tumultuous relationship. I made it clear that I had no interest in trying to pretend to be friends with someone who I'd never been friends with in the first place. And then I disconnected him.

Period. My truth. My power. Felt great!

When it comes to boundaries, remember that it's your space. Your body. Your emotions. Your life. Your energy. Protect all of it as if your life depends on it. Because it does.

Chapter 16

Owning Your Whole Story

When we deny our story, it defines us. When we own our story,
we get to write the ending.
—Brené Brown, remarks at South by Southwest Interactive
Conference, 2016

Why do we hide who we are? Why do we feel it is necessary to be an actor on the stage of our very own life? We put on hats, play roles, say things we don't mean, and do things to appease others. Never has hiding behind false pretense been so prevalent than right now. The expectations of what we should have accomplished by the time we are thirty; the responses we are expected to have on certain social issues; what we can and cannot say regarding our political beliefs; the way we look, eat, carry ourselves—it's all out there, across all media and all platforms. Everyone believes they have a story to tell and that everyone else should hear it. So we post, we filter, we create avatars; we offer unsolicited advice and uninformed opinions; we react and compare; like or not like; follow and unfriend. It's a bit haywire.

I do believe we all have a story to tell; that's why I'm writing this book. But if what I share is not the real story, the whole story, the good-the-bad-and-the-ugly story, I don't believe it's worth hearing. Because filtered stories aren't real. I know, because I hid behind a false narrative—ashamed of revealing the parts of me that I was certain didn't fit into the norm (whatever that means), or might expose me as not being good enough, less than, a fraud. My truth was suppressed not by a made-up story of who I was or a pack of purposely made-up lies about my past, but by omission. I got good at it. Making up a truth (also known as lying) isn't that far off from leaving solemn parts of yourself out of the story. Whether you make up a new story that you believe fills the expectations of others or leave yourself out of your truth altogether, you are practicing two cardinal sins of self-love: self-rejection and self-abandonment.

Letting Go of Shame

Shame. *Ick*. Just typing the word makes me want to run and hide. Shame is defined as "a painful feeling of humiliation or distress caused by the consciousness of wrong or foolish behavior."[1] No wonder it ruins lives. We all at one time or another have tortured ourselves and hidden our shame, trying to compensate for it in ways that are mostly unhealthy, and shoving the feelings and experiences in a box, totally denying them or, worse, numbing them (also in the unhealthiest self-abandoning ways).

Acclaimed marriage and family therapist Dr. Nadine Macaluso specializes in what is known as relational trauma, recognized by the World Health Organization as complex PTSD (C-PTSD). Much of her work and therapy are rooted in overcoming shame, especially shame that develops in early childhood as a response to parental abandonment, neglect, and abuse.

I learn so much from Dr. Nae's Instagram posts alone, which I highly recommend following. She describes shame as the feeling that you are bad, broken, or unworthy of love. "It leads to a fear of being seen," she writes on her blog. "As adults, shame manifests in feelings of loneliness, helplessness, hopelessness, anxiety, and depression. Adults experience shame when they ruminate about their personal defects, focus on their inadequacies, believe they are not worthy of love, or do not believe that they can impact their future. Shame is a circuit breaker for joy, pleasure, connection, and vitality."[2]

For many of us, shame seems to be an accepted part of life. We are afraid we will be outed for being not good enough—frauds in the world of people who have done everything right, as if nobody else in the world has ever had bad things happen to them, had bad people happen to them, or been guilty of a trespass now and again. Or made a bad decision. God forbid!

I used to feel piles of shame about the fact that the highest degree that I hold is a GED. I went to college briefly but never finished. Most of my friends and peers had a college degree, so I feared that my lack of education and similar college experiences would render me an outsider or make them believe I wasn't up to snuff to hang with them. The saddest part of this assumption was that I believed my life and career wouldn't be great with "just" my GED.

Here is one thing about avoiding conversations and pretending all the time: it's exhausting. And sometimes exhaustion causes you to wave the white flag of surrender, which can be the best thing to do in certain situations. "Surrender" means to stop fighting, and the word itself gets a bad rap. Many people assume surrender is giving up or giving in, but that is not the type of surrender I'm talking about. When you surrender to an experience or emotion, you stop trying to prevent or control it. I stopped treating my story and my truth as my bully and stopped being a victim to it. It was a game changer.

Normally, when someone would ask me what college I graduated from, this would trigger shame for me, causing me to try to brush past the question by quickly answering it with something like "I didn't finish college" and then trying to take the focus off of me in hopes of preventing them from digging any deeper into my educational background. But that always made me feel like I was hiding the truth, which is that I barely went to the college that I briefly attended. Even more, I barely went to high school. I had so much turmoil going on in my teenage years, school was the last thing on my mind.

But one day I decided to embrace my story, and eventually I had absolutely no reservations about telling people that not only do I not have a college degree, but the highest degree I received was a GED. Rather than hiding from this story, I embraced it fully because it is mine, and it's the only one I've got—and will ever have. And being more open about the truth of my story lifted any sense of shame I had been feeling prior to embracing my story. It helped reenergize my power container.

Once I began owning my story, I began to see the value in how much I had actually survived and accomplished despite my circumstances. I began to feel much more powerful. Surrendering to my reality helped me discover the uniqueness and power of my story for the first time, and I wanted nothing more than to own it. My education and the choices I made in my education journey are a part of me—and I love me.

Don't get me wrong. When I meet someone new, I don't lead with it, like "Hi, I'm Jenna. I have a GED and no college degree." But I don't hide from it either. I don't change the subject if someone is telling stories about the old days at football games at Clemson or feel intimidated when I meet someone with a master's or PhD. When this part of my story is relevant in conversation, I now have zero reservation about sharing. And every time I share it, I feel prouder of my accomplishments. My career and life success are in spite of a lack of degrees, connections, or family support. Believe me, I own that as hard as an Olympian owns her medal. And because I own my story, it has absolutely zero power over me. In the words of Marianne Williamson, "The moment of surrender is not when life is over, it's when it begins."[3]

Shame Is a Self-Limiting Belief

For many years, I thought of my GED as my defect, my inadequacy, my reason for not being worthy of love and friendship or connection with those "more educated" than I am. Dr. Nae explains that when we ruminate like I did, shame-based statements such as these result:

- I can't relate to people.
- I am a failure.
- Nobody could love me.
- I am unlovable.
- I can't do it.
- I don't believe in myself.
- I am not worthy.
- I don't deserve positive things.
- I can't make mistakes.
- I have to be perfect (to be loved, accepted, etc.).
- I'm not good enough; I'm not enough.[4]

Partaking in this negative chatter, internalizing shame, allowing it to define us, and suppressing our stories are examples of what is known in psychology circles as *self-abandonment*. Nobody talks about this! It is so huge and makes so much sense, especially if you are trying with all your might to love yourself and can't seem to figure out how.

According to an article on the website of the National Alliance on Mental Illness (NAMI), "Essentially, self-abandonment is when you reject, suppress, or ignore part of yourself in real-time." Put another way, "you have a need or desire you want to meet, and (often on the spot) you make the decision *not* to meet it."[5]

Valuing Your Uniqueness

In Part II, I talk about self-sabotage and the things we do that prevent us from loving ourselves. Essentially, all of them are practices of self-abandonment. For example, you've just come home from a day at work, feeling beat up, when a friend calls. You want to take a warm bath and to hit the sack early, but she needs your ear. You agree to meet up with her for a drink to listen to her problems, despite your original plans to take some quiet time. Or your credit card statement balance is off the rails, and when your brother asks you to spot him a fifty, you hand it over, even though you need to start paying down your own debt. Or you really want to become a hairdresser, but your friends think that is a lame job, so you decide to enroll in a local community college, paying tuition toward an unknown degree. This is *self-abandonment*! We must stop abandoning ourselves by no longer abandoning our own stories. That means we must eliminate any shame that surrounds that story. Tall order, for sure.

It can take years of therapy to deal with shame and to stop using self-abandonment as a coping mechanism, so of course I recommend therapy for anyone who deals with the same issue. In her blog post "The Relationship between Shame and Complex PTSD," Dr. Nae, herself a survivor of relational trauma and shame, shares some advice on how to begin tackling shame so we can shut it out for good. For personal growth to happen, she urges us to accept ourselves and be open to change. This is the way to generate self-love and self-validation. We need to develop a "self-affirming identity," whereby we become empowered to own all our imperfections and differences.[6]

"Learn to value your uniqueness and differentness—these are inherent qualities that set you apart and must be recognized and savored by you," Dr. Nae writes. "Personal validation creates a secure positive sense of self." To do this, she advises we build a robust inner witness that can observe the programmed thoughts of our inner critic and choose not to believe them. "Cultivating an inner witness is the skill of being present in the moment," she says.[7]

Eckhart Tolle, in his book *The Power of Now*, also talks about witnessing your thoughts to remain in present-moment awareness. I so believe in the power of the present moment. My journey has been filled with teachings and practices by masters of Zen Buddhism, mindfulness, and meditation, all of which teach how to become aware in the present, rooted deeply in the now. When it comes to building my inner witness, the one who guards and polices the negative chatter, self-abandonment, and self-loathing threatening my self-love, I have learned to calibrate my energy in various ways. My energy is my guide, my medicine, and my beacon of strength when it comes to fighting shame. Shame can be felt energetically in the body, which is why being in tune with your energy is a critical component of dealing with shame. Our physical energy can provide hints and reveal our degree of shame, and it can help us stay in touch with it at all times so we can try to mitigate its effects on us.

Bret Lyon, cocreator and codirector of the Center for Healing Shame, explains how shame affects our emotional and physical health when he writes, "Shame is a binding emotion, latching onto and interfering with the free flow of other emotions, such as anger, fear and grief. Trungpa Rinpoche suggests that Energy + Story = Emotion. Most emotions have a natural rhythm and path to expression. When they are fully expressed, energy is released. We can drop the story and just feel the energy. I believe that emotions are expressions of our life energy. If they are bound with shame, however, they cannot complete."[8]

Daniel Siegel and others have spoken of the importance of having a coherent narrative—a story that describes and explains what happened in your life and makes some sense out of it. "Shame is an incredibly powerful and compelling coherent narrative," says Lyon. "Whatever happened, it was my fault."[9]

We want to complete our life energy, don't we? Just like we want our story to be complete and not hidden or overwrought with the cancer of shame. By understanding the concepts discussed here, I have been able to calibrate my energy to take control of my shame and make owning my story a continual practice of self-love. I hope you find these ideas helpful and that they inspire you to bear witness to your own shame.

The Power of an Ugly Story

You, too, may have a hurt or struggle that you let define you in some way, whether it influences your choices and decisions, the belief system you have, or the people with whom you surround yourself. By suppressing hurtful stories, they continue to have a hold on us subconsciously. We internalize them. This is a natural defense mechanism for surviving—not necessarily the trauma itself (although that can be the case) but the *shame* that develops as a result of the trauma.

Whether it's past abuse, mental health issues, addiction, or a previous criminal offense, shame is always involved. If you try to hide these stories, they will only end up owning you in the end, because shame is an insidious poison that will destroy your ability to love others, to allow others to love you, and most of all, to love yourself.

The only way to own our stories, to see the value in our experiences, mistakes, and shortcomings, is through overcoming shame. We shouldn't own only the good stories of our lives. We should own the failures, the regrets, and the poor choices we've made or the wrongdoing that others have inflicted on us.

I'd like you to think about the power in any part of your own story that is ugly. I know there is power in the ugly parts not just because I decided to own my story and come out of victimhood but because I've also seen many other brave women show their vulnerable sides. And many of them who've come out with their stories have felt a much bigger impact on their lives than I did when I owned my story. The Bravo TV franchise *The Real Housewives* is one of my "guilty" pleasures. Just go with me here for a second. Some of the women on this show have been able to use their platform to release the shame connected to their most traumatic circumstances. In part, my decision to share my story and my journey to loving myself more was inspired by others, including some of the housewives, who experienced or relived trauma or humiliation on the show and told the world what happened to them, only to reduce the stigma for the rest of us.

- Bethenny Frankel of *The Real Housewives of New York* opened up about having a traumatic childhood.
- Taylor Armstrong of *The Real Housewives of Beverly Hills* shared her story of domestic abuse.
- Elizabeth Lyn Vargas from *The Real Housewives of Orange County* has shared details about growing up in a religious cult that was run by her grandmother, where she was repeatedly sexually abused.
- Kim Richards of *The Real Housewives of Beverly Hills* has been openly struggling with drug addiction.

And that's just the short list!

These picture-perfect women stopped suppressing and pretending and showed the world that almost all people, no matter their walk in life, experience shame. They normalized it. They shared my belief that it is a choice to let your shame bind you or set you—and others—free. I'm sure you know which choice I've made for my life. I hope you'll do the same for yours.

JOURNALING SUGGESTION

What Parts of Your Story Have You Kept Hidden?

- Think about and write down any stories you have that make you feel bad about yourself and that you might not feel comfortable sharing with others.
- Write down what you believe others would think of you if they were to learn this story.
- Has this story held you back in your life in any way? Write down how.
- What do you think would happen if you started to take ownership over this story and take back your power?

PART IV

The Business of Self-Love: Transform Your Career, Increase Your Wealth, Go for Your Entrepreneurial Dream

> Your self-worth determines your net worth.
> —Suze Orman, Instagram post, November 6, 2018

For decades women in business have been portrayed as everything from the dutiful, wide-eyed *Mad Men*-ish secretary and the big-haired, not-to-be-taken-seriously working girl to the childless corporate executive spinster and assistant-eating ice queen who wears Prada. Stereotypes abound! We've been told to "act like men," and when we do, we are "bitches." We've been taught to break the glass ceiling, to dance on it, and even to shatter it for good. Where in the world are *we*—the person, the talent, the spirit—in all of this? The hyper-effort and concentration placed on fitting in, acting "right," and finding the right persona when it comes to the business sides of our lives (yes, managing a household and a personal checking account is also business) is, in my opinion, complete *self-abandonment*, which, as we know, is *not* self-love.

Some women use work as a way of proving their value, and that is not self-love either. Neither are the following:

- Being in debt, overspending, or buying things you cannot afford to please or impress others
- Not having enough in savings for at least a six-month emergency fund
- Overspending on others (children, parents, friends, philanthropy) when you do not have your own finances in order
- Remaining overly dependent on others for financial security

Fear, lack of confidence, and self-sacrificing; these are just a few reasons women don't pursue their career endeavors or opt themselves out before they move up the chain of command. They are also the reasons many women find themselves living beyond their means, not putting financial fitness first. Perhaps they are filling a void by spending money or are chasing perfection by investing in countless products that promise a new "reality" for the imperfect woman.

When you feel good, you benefit everyone around you. When you feel overworked, are underpaid, are in a dead-end job, don't have the time or energy to pursue your passion or build your side hustle, are in debt, live paycheck to paycheck, or spend money frivolously to keep up with the Joneses, you invite stress into your life. That energy spent tossing and turning and indulging in too many martinis needs to be reallocated to the bank of self-love. If self-love were a bank, then lamenting over a boss, living in regret over the endeavor you never attempted, or the half-finished oil painting in your basement will leave you with insufficient sums in no time.

> That energy spent tossing and turning and indulging in too many martinis needs to be reallocated to the bank of self-love.

I don't know many people who equate self-love with work, entrepreneurship, or mastering a financial software program, but to me, mastering the business aspect of one's life is an act of not only self-love but self-respect and self-actualization. This is the business of self-love, and we dissect it throughout the following chapters. Chapter 17 discusses self-love and careers; Chapter 18 talks about self-love and financial fitness. Sometimes they run parallel, and other times they feed one another like rivers.

Chapter 17

What Are You Worth to Your Employer?

I've known many incredibly smart, skilled women who were far more effective at their jobs than their male counterparts but who got paid far less because they didn't value themselves. I've known women who were capable of higher positions than they had but who didn't know their value and settled for support roles instead. You determine your value. Everyone else just reflects back the value you have for yourself.

Why do women naturally downplay their value, while men do the opposite? The reasons could fill a library of works, but the three I've encountered most in my experience, and that are directly related to our ability to love ourselves, are the following: lack of self-promotion, the doormat dilemma (taking on self-limiting tasks), and focusing on the wrong (nonpromotable) tasks. Let me ask you four questions that will help you avoid these traps.

Question 1: Are You Willing to Become a Self-Promoter?

Motivated to escape the home of my tormenting father, I was incredibly hungry to earn my own money. At fourteen years old, I submitted an application to work at a fast-food restaurant, despite the minimum age requirement of fifteen. I got called in for an interview. Driving me to the interview, my father gave me some invaluable advice. "It's very easy to get any job you want," he told me. "You just have to go in confidently, and as soon as you meet them, in those first seconds, shake their hand firmly and look them in the eyes." He also advised that I ask questions, to interview them as much as they were interviewing me. It's a great tactic to maintain your position of self-power when pursuing a position.

I got the job. The immediate positive reinforcement programmed me to always approach a job with complete confidence, knowing that how I felt about my abilities and the confidence that I conveyed would make all the difference among my future competition and combat any self-doubt that would creep in. I also learned that regardless of the listed requirements for the job, as long as I remained confident in my ability to get the job done, I wouldn't let my lack of experience hold me back from going for it.

This isn't the norm. You may have heard the statistic that was made famous by Sheryl Sandberg in her book *Lean In* and repeated in *The Confidence Code* and news articles, which says that men apply for a job when they meet only 60 percent of the qualifications, but women tend to apply only if they meet 100 percent of them. This is indicative of the power of our self-limiting beliefs. Women feel as if they need to tick 100 percent of the job requirement boxes before they even apply!

Because of the lessons I learned at an early age, I was able to move further in my career than I would have otherwise. When pursuing a job, instead of checking requirement boxes (which often include a college degree, or in the case of my first job, an age requirement), I envision myself doing the job or not. "Am I capable?" replaces "Am I qualified?"

The jury is still out on why women are averse to self-promotion. It could be because of societal norms or fear of being perceived as cocky or tooting our horns, or that gender roles have taught us to play it small and be humble. In an interview I did with Stephanie Ritz, a career strategist, on an episode of my YouTube video series and podcast *The*

Jenna Banks Show, Stephanie says, "Saying, 'This is what I did,' to make sure that the key team members [know] what you're doing, is really important because . . . this is something that men have no problem with—going out there and saying, 'Hey, I did this. I led this team. I got this contract.' . . . [Women] don't want to be braggy; [they] don't want to be that one who is discluding anyone else."[1]

Regardless of why we do it, we need to stop. Undermining our abilities and not taking our shot blocks our ability to self-love. The worst of all is that the more we don't play up our gifts, the less we believe they exist. We can actually start to believe our own lies: *We are not enough*, despite the facts pointing to the contrary. According to a recent National Bureau of Economic Research working paper, women consistently rated their performance on a test lower than men did, even though both groups had the same average score.[2]

Unfortunately, our self-love resolve is constantly tested in the business arena. I have a friend who now works as a district manager for a very large public company. She makes more than a lot of men I know. She lives in a gorgeous, expensive high-rise condo in the city with an insane view overlooking skyscrapers. It wasn't too long ago when she was much lower in rank. She'd been working at this company for years, working many late nights and weekends on behalf of her department so she'd be seen as a "good team player." She assumed that one day she'd be rewarded for her efforts, except that day never came. Instead, her bosses were promoted for the good work "the department" was doing, and she realized she'd been serving as nothing more than a doormat.

Finally frustrated and at her wit's end, she called a meeting with human resources, fully prepared to resign if she wasn't recognized with title and pay for her work. Instead of waiting around for those to recognize her work like she had been doing, she went into self-promotion mode, listing and proving the various wins she had scored for her department. Human resources had no idea. She walked into that meeting ready to quit if they weren't going to do something about it.

Today, she is highly respected at her organization, is constantly being promoted into bigger roles, and has nearly made it to the top echelon of the company. And to think all it took was that one big step forward on her part to speak up and stand up for her worth, promote herself, and be willing to leave if she wasn't valued as much as she valued herself.

When I was in my twenties, I was recruited as a sales and marketing manager for an office products company, reporting directly to the CEO. The salary wasn't as lucrative as I had hoped, but it was worth the exchange for the title and level of opportunity. After a year, I realized the scope of the job surpassed my compensation, and after doing some research, I discovered I was underpaid by almost double compared to what our competitors paid. Knowledge is power indeed. I could have allowed my lack of a college education to make me feel like I should have just been grateful for the opportunity and accept what I was given. But that would have been a self-imposed limiting belief. Instead, I focused on all the skills that I brought to the table. I called a meeting with my boss, first rehearsing my negotiation bullet points. I'm glad I did.

Some people see negotiation as an art, and my boss certainly was one of them. I see negotiation as an opportunity to communicate your value to yourself and others. I set the bar high for a pay rate increase to be more on par with our competitors, which resulted in a 50 percent pay increase (just what I wanted). A former boss had told me, "Jenna, business owners always have money; they just act like they don't." Since receiving that tip long ago, I always kept it front of mind when negotiating. Their money isn't my concern. My money is my concern.

Question 2: Do You Have the Courage to Avoid the Doormat Dilemma?

In Chapter 12, I tell you the story of how I didn't make a coffee run for the company president who was visiting our offices from India. Believe it or not, taking on hostess roles at work skews the company's perception of your value. When you are trying to gain respect and get promotions, engaging in "housework" at the office, especially when men are asking for it, can do a ton of disservice to your reputation and your self-esteem. Helping out with serving food at the office, fetching coffee for everyone—these are surefire ways of becoming less of a company door buster and more of doormat. (Do you see men doing these activities? No.)

Don't be the office doormat. It gets you nowhere and works against you. In the 2014 edition of her book *Nice Girls Don't Get the Corner Office*, executive coach Lois P. Frankel advises women that if the boss makes the request in front of a group, to "practice saying in a neutral, unemotional way, 'I think I'll pass, since I did it last time.'"[3] This enables you to gently but firmly remind the group that your time—and your value—is being mismanaged.

Question 3: Are You Willing to Say No to Nonpromotable Tasks?

Being focused is a commendable trait, especially in the world of business. But being focused on the wrong things—well, that's the pathway to the windowless cubicle. The last thing we want to do is spend our energy on tasks that aren't going to showcase our potential and that are likely not the things that get us closer to our goals.

The 2017 issue of the *American Economic Review* published research that found that women are more likely to volunteer for and get asked to do tasks that are not going to help them rise in their careers. The study modeled the personal cost of taking on a task others are reluctant to do, such as writing a report, serving on a committee, or planning a holiday party. Under time pressure, someone had to volunteer for the task, or the group would lose out on money. If no one volunteered, each person would be paid $1.00. But if someone volunteered, that volunteer who saved the day received $1.25, while the other group members received $2.00. After ten rounds, women were 48 percent more likely than men to volunteer for a task that would financially benefit the rest of the group more than them. Overall, the participants equally were not jumping to volunteer, but as the clock wound down, a woman was more likely to take one for the team and do the undesirable task.[4]

These are staggering statistics! There are times in everyone's life when self-sacrifice is a noble gesture whose benefits outweigh the cost to the individual. But to routinely be altruistic *in the workplace* at our own expense is professional self-sabotage. If you are interested in career advancement and professional growth, you need to practice self-love by minimizing the number of tasks you take on that will not help you achieve the next rung up the ladder.

Question 4: Can You Practice Self-Compassion in Your Professional Life?

Self-criticism and self-loathing build barriers to career advancement that you might not even be aware of. When you're focused on career-climbing, it's easy to let the inner critic take center stage, telling you how unworthy or dumb you are, as opposed to embracing the inner cheerleader who gives you kudos when you are doing a good job throughout your day.

Self-abandonment in the career world comes in many forms, including focusing on negative moments and not celebrating the positive ones. We find little time to review small victories, take stock of the good we have done in one day, or look at setbacks as learning opportunities. But we do focus heavily on the passed-over promotions, minor missteps, or failed outcomes and internalize them until we condemn ourselves to the status of less than zero. I have had many friends who only valued themselves if their bosses or coworkers gave them external kudos. Remember: External validation that feeds our internal compass is a huge self-love saboteur!

We've talked a lot about self-compassion, and when it comes to our careers, this is where the rubber meets the road. Neuroscientists have discovered a direct link between self-compassion, resilience, and success. Dr. Bryan Robinson, *Forbes* contributor and author of *#Chill: Turn Off Your Job and Turn On Your Life*, writes, "Self-love and self-affirmations serve as 'cognitive expanders,' allowing us to talk to ourselves the way we might speak to someone else so that the judgment voice isn't the only story we tell ourselves. As a result, self-love provides the fuel that boosts our moods, job performance, and achievement."[5]

I do this all the time and never knew it had a formal scientific name. Because of the reading I do in the spirituality category, I recognize this practice of self-affirmation as *loving-kindness*, a Buddhist principle that directs compassion and benevolence first toward oneself and then toward others. American Buddhist nun Pema Chödrön, in her book *When Things Fall Apart*, calls this *maitrl*—a Sanskrit word meaning "loving-kindness and an unconditional friendship with ourselves."[6] When we aspire to do great work, whether in our jobs, attaining a promotion, or starting our own company, there are ways to make sure we evoke the power of loving-kindness with ourselves, boosting our worth and value, making it likelier we promote instead of downplay ourselves.

When it comes to showing myself loving-kindness while I'm wearing my business cap, I like to think outside the box by practicing some of the following:

- *Put my achievements on the record.* A tangible and practical way of doing this is by adding notable productive moments to my resume or profile on LinkedIn. Regarding our resumes, we tend to list only the career highlights like job titles or creating new divisions, but what about the profit gains this quarter or the new hiring you just led? These are important value adds that we tend to forget if we don't record them when they happen. Put them on the record, and feel that surge of self-love!

- *Invest in my professional development.* I've said this before, but investing in yourself is key in communicating to your spirit that you love yourself and you are worth that love. The same goes for investing in developing your interests. Whether it's a summer writer's workshop, a networking event across the country, or finally signing up for a seminar with your favorite thought leader, taking the time to enhance your knowledge—and your connections—not only breaks up the monotony but exposes you to new ideas and new facets to who you are and would like to be. Plus, how can you hope that other people—an employer, business investor—will see your worth and invest in you if you aren't even willing to spend your own money investing in yourself? When you invest in yourself, you build up your sense of self-confidence and self-worth. And that inner worth really shines through to the outside world.

- *Find your joy at work.* As Anita Moorjani teaches us in her *New York Times* best-selling book *Dying to Be Me,* our purpose on this earth is to express who we are, to love who we are, and to have fun with life. Work should not have to feel like a death sentence. Don't get me wrong: Even people who love their jobs will have days when they just want to ditch it all and live in a tiny house somewhere in the Rocky Mountains. After a long day, I reflect on the various encounters I have had—the email exchanges, the food I ate, the meetings I attended, the joke I heard, and so on. And then I write a list (even a short one), of the tiny moments of joy I felt and experienced. This is a great sanity saver if you are feeling trapped in a dead-end job and are pressed to stay there to make ends meet.

Defend Your Value

Back before I had my own company, I landed a job as a division manager for a consumer products company. I was tasked with growing and managing my department, which at the time I was hired brought in approximately $3 million in annual revenue for the company. While the base pay was menial, my compensation plan included a highly incentivized bonus plan. Because I saw tremendous potential for growth within this market, and I was confident in my capabilities to achieve such growth, I was agreeable to the package. Growth soon followed, and I began making more money than my bosses anticipated. After a year, the executive management team told me they needed to revise my comp plan. The old bait and switch!

I reminded the team that my making good money meant so were they! I didn't need them; I stuck around solely for the financial opportunity. If they changed my plan, I would no longer be incentivized to stay. When I told them this truth, I wasn't emotional or defensive; it was just business as usual. This was about money: for me and for them. The name of the game was to uphold and defend my worth—an act of self-love.

Of course, they backed right down, and the "issue" was never brought up again. Part of communicating your worth is the willingness to walk away. Just like my friend who works for the Fortune 500 company did when she went into her HR department that pivotal day, I was fully ready to move on if they were willing to devalue and undermine me—not to mention insult my intelligence by trying to take advantage of me.

If I had accepted devaluation, where would the limit be? When would they stop? What message would I have sent them? You must know and defend your value so that others know how to treat you. You have to first value yourself if you want to be valued by others. By the time I left the company, my department was bringing in over $12 million in annual revenue. And I know that my skills and abilities were what helped bring this growth to fruition.

We all want to have dignity and be treated with dignity, and I have found that I have never felt more proud and more dignified than when

I achieved self-sufficiency, sometimes in my career, sometimes in my personal finances, sometimes both at the same time. The relationship between self-love and self-sufficiency is reciprocal: The more self-love you have, the more you achieve; the more you achieve, the more self-love you have.

JOURNALING SUGGESTION

Getting Ready to Promote Yourself

Now is a great time to check in with yourself and see how you feel about applying for jobs as well as promoting yourself.

- How have you approached applying for jobs or promoting yourself up until this point? Have you eliminated yourself from applying for jobs if you didn't meet 100 percent of the listed requirements? Do you feel like your work and accomplishments are well known at your company? Could your career benefit from some self-promotion?
- What are some of the things you've learned in this chapter that you could apply to better serve you and your career?
- What nonpromotable tasks do you think would be good for you to stop doing at work?
- When you catch yourself putting yourself down for something you did or didn't do at work, what would be a better way to handle yourself with your internal dialog?

Chapter 18

Putting the *Fine* Back in Finances

Being financially fit is extremely beneficial for your well-being and your sense of self-worth. But it is also one of the hardest aspects of our lives to control. A survey produced by Capital One in 2020 found that 77 percent of Americans are anxious about their financial situation, 58 percent believe their finances control their lives rather than them controlling their finances, and 52 percent have difficulty controlling worries about money.[1] Add to that the reality that finances are at the top of most complications between life partners and, for far too many, a source of a person's self-worth.

In a world where we are more likely to ask a stranger at a party, "What do you do for a living?" than "What are your interests?" it is difficult not to wrap our self-worth in how much money we make, the car we drive, or the amount of savings in our IRAs. Money might be the root of all evil, but it is also the Weedwacker to the flowers of our self-love. Whether we chase money to validate our own worth, spend money to prove ourselves to others, or live beyond our means to provide for our families (e.g., saving for the kids' colleges we cannot afford, buying luxury and name brand everything because that's the norm around our town, taking expensive vacations because "we deserve it," or buying products that we believe will compensate for our imperfections and shortcomings), we are using money as a veil. While we may feel we are filling our bank with Benjamins, we are losing the only funds that can truly sustain us: the ones in our self-love bank.

Creating a new relationship with ourselves on our self-love journey requires that we create a new relationship with our finances and transform how we view the purpose of money in the first place.

Don't Be a Victim of Financial Self-Sabotage

A general definition of financial fitness is to have the money you need, when you need it. I found a discussion of the ways that a lack of self-love can hinder our ability to become financially fit on the blog *Broke Generation*.[2] Here's my interpretation of several ideas that really resonated with me:

- *Spending to feel better:* Some people grab Cherry Garcia on a bad day; others throw a blanket over their heads and binge-watch *90 Day Fiancé.* Some go on an online shopping spree. It's all about self-soothing, and, hey, it happens. Forgive yourself, and make a conscious effort to pause in the moment, recognize what you are doing, and phone a friend instead. What you should do instead is to show yourself loving-kindness and compassion. Deep down, you know the hit of dopamine you'll get from that next shopping spree will end in a shame spiral when the bill collector robocalls.
- *Unconscious spending that is self-sabotage:* I could write a book on this topic alone. We start to make headway, and then—*boom*— we do something to set us back and don't even realize it until it's too late. It's as if we are afraid of what would happen if we actually succeeded.
- *Buying to impress or copy others:* Anyone who says yes to Pellegrino when tap water is just fine, this one's for you. You are enough without the labels or picking up the tab. All I can see

is a lack of self-love when I encounter someone toting a Louis Vuitton purse while complaining about being in credit card debt. Be conscious when you are seeking validation and acceptance through spending.

- *We don't think we're worthy of financial independence:* We tell ourselves that we're just not cut out to be one of the "haves" in the world—and that mentality turns into habitual spending and acts as a self-fulfilling prophecy. If you think you are not worthy of living like "everyone else" because you attained a GED instead of a PhD, or you're recovering from an addiction, or you still believe things that were said to you by your parents when you were young, understand that none of that self-talk exists in reality! You *are* deserving because you are a soul living on this earth, and you *can* and should do everything possible to become a responsible spender and saver.

Overcoming this kind of thinking isn't easy. In my twenties, I didn't really care to focus on my finances. I obtained decent-sized credit limits on my credit cards and tapped them when I wanted to go on a shopping spree. I found myself drowning in debt from credit cards and a car payment that was way over my pay grade, along with other forms of gratuitous purchases. I felt suffocated by daily money stress. Eventually, to save my mental well-being, I filed for bankruptcy at just twenty-seven years old. It's impossible to feel in your power with this kind of constant money stress weighing your energy down. Instead of owning our power, we are owing it all over the place!

Surrendering to bankruptcy was humbling and incredibly relieving. I accepted that I was going to pay a major price with a huge hit to my credit score for many years, along with the inability to easily borrow again far into the future. I remained accountable for my actions and fought hard against playing victim. Crawling my way up from ground zero was a task I decided to consciously focus my energy on, while turning away the shame that was attempting to seep into my self-love bank. I became interested in how to get in the driver's seat of my financial life. I wanted to be financially fit! Thankfully I discovered books and videos from Suze Orman, world-renowned financial advisor, and set my sights on getting financially healthy and eventually wealthy.

Taking On Financial Responsibility for Others

Caregiving is a responsibility that most of us cannot avoid. From the cost of parenting young children to taking care of aging parents to putting children through college, many of us at one point in our lives will have someone depending on us. This can be so taxing on our capacity for self-love that I've dedicated an entire chapter to caregiving. But part of caring for others is sometimes to also take financial responsibility for them, and that not only can be stressful but also can result in misspending for all the wrong reasons.

When you're stressing yourself financially to get your kids into private school, college, excessive sports activities, or giving money to your family members when it puts a financial stress on you, you are not doing yourself any favors. Everyone around you benefits when your energy is strong. You have to put yourself and your financial fitness first. Only then can you provide a solid foundation from which to give love to others, including your kids.

As a parent myself, I recall the borderline obsession many other parents had about college. I don't need to tell you about the insanity that getting kids into college evokes in even the most sane people. I thought the high-profile corruption of Hollywood actors committing fraud and bribery to ensure their kids got into the "right" college would be a wake-up call, but still people around the country are going into insurmountable debt—the kind of debt that will bury them for life—in order for their kids to have a shot, not only at a college education but at the "right" one.

Suze Orman, in her signature style, calls parents out on their BS. When commenting on a survey by T. Rowe Price that reported 68 percent of parents overall and 75 percent of millennials thought saving for their kids' college was a more important priority than saving for their own retirement, she wrote, "Are you nuts? Your 20s and 30s are when saving [for] retirement gives you a huge advantage: decades when your money can grow. Waiting until your 40s to get serious about retirement saving means losing out on so many valuable years of compound growth."[3]

From Financial Folly to Financial Fitness to Financial Freedom: My Entrepreneurial Journey

I had to stop lying to myself. I had to stop using money to fill voids, to prove things about myself, to make friends, to cover up deficiencies, to feel like I was "enough." I needed to love myself more—more than the external validation, more than the false pretenses, and way more than the fleeting highs I would feel when I spent money that I didn't have or spent money I had *but spent it for the wrong reasons*. Once I did that, my life not only turned around; it reached a turning point I never dreamed possible. Activating the business of self-love in my personal finances directly correlated with my career trajectory. That is why these two topics are discussed throughout this chapter. There

Activating the business of self-love in my personal finances directly correlated with my career trajectory.

is a time when they will intersect and feed one another like rivers, because among other places, self-esteem and confidence come from financial independence, and financial independence opens pathways and opportunities that our newfound confidence can seize.

Post-bankruptcy, I made it a mental game to see how many points I could get my credit score to go up based on the new self-empowering and self-loving decisions I made about my money. I knew it would take time, but my goal was to be in a position where I could begin to buy property and start growing my wealth.

I started building my savings, ensuring I always had a six-month emergency fund in a savings account. Just knowing that I had a cushion of safety eased my money stress. This freed up so much energy and released me from the negative energy that held me captive.

I moved on to saving even more, keeping my money in an account that paid a decent interest rate so that my money could earn money. I took advantage of my employer's 401(k) option, investing as much of my paycheck as I could afford and ensuring I got every penny of their matching options. I paid attention to my 401(k) investments and took an interest in what stocks, ETFs, and mutual funds were performing well. I vowed never to pay credit card interest again and flipped that script to ensure I would instead get paid interest on my money and earned cash rewards on credit cards that I paid off each and every month. Each empowering financial step I took made me feel good about myself, which resulted in increased confidence and self-worth. As my self-worth grew, so did, as Suze Orman says, my net worth.

Eventually, I was able to buy two properties in Atlanta, which I turned into Airbnb properties, both earning a profit each month, all while building equity and my wealth. As my savings grew, I had more freedom regarding my work, where I lived, and how I could spend my time. No longer tethered to debt, I was able to leave my rent-controlled apartment in Santa Monica after seventeen years and venture to the San Francisco Bay area. Because I was free to roam the country, I could quit my cushy corporate job and start my own business. Without having the savings to lean on, I would never have been able to take that leap of faith.

Selling Brand Spirit

When I left my safe corporate job near the city I had lived almost my entire adult life in, I had no idea what I would do. But I just knew that I did not feel good in my body when I was at work. It felt toxic. I had a really unsettled feeling, like something wasn't right, and it was time to make a major change in my life. Honestly, soon after quitting, life wasn't pretty. For around a month, I was depressed and then worried and anxious. I gave myself some time to think, heal, and sit with my fear. It was okay, I trusted my instinct, but I won't tell you I didn't have bouts of panic. After soul-searching and allowing the noise in my head to exit my mind and body, I was clear. I decided I would attempt to start my own business again. My goal was to feel good, love what I did for work, and live the life I wanted to live.

I'd had my own company before, selling promotional products to clients in the entertainment industry, working for movie and TV studios such as Sony Pictures, Paramount, and USA Network. And I loved doing that. Before that, I was a partner in a board game company that I cofounded. One of our biggest accomplishments was getting a licensing deal for our game that resulted in millions of units being made for, and included in, Arby's kids' meals.

All my entrepreneurial experience was incredibly valuable to me, so I already knew what it was like to start a business from the ground up. And I already had plenty of experience in the marketing products business (promotional products). But I had an idea to do it differently. Before I started my company in 2012, most companies that sold marketing products did it the old-fashioned way. They would employ sales reps who would have a base of clients they met with in person, taking them to lunches and driving them to their offices for meetings.

My hunch was that busy millennial managers did not want to leave their office to buy marketing products. Selling trends were moving online, so I set up a website and learned the latest online marketing practices. My very first client was NASDAQ! Moving online made my business national instead of regional and allowed for more active contact and relationship building through emails, web content, blogging, and online networking/social media.

During the first few years of running the business, I bootstrapped it, working largely on my own. But I began to feel a bit burned out after working long hours every day and weekends. So I set out to build an affordable support team. Sales grew nicely each year while I began to work less and less in the business, relying on my team for most of the daily business tasks. The new free time allowed me to go explore the world and travel more than I ever had in the past.

In 2019, I was asked to be a guest speaker at a B2B marketing convention in Los Angeles. I'd never been a speaker before and have always had a major fear of public speaking. I decided to say yes and worry about how I'd face this fear head on when the time came. On the heels of that speaking offer, I received a postcard in the mail inviting me to a seminar on how to sell your business. I really hadn't been thinking about selling my business at that time, but because I always invested in myself and felt this would be a topic that would enrich me, I went to the seminar. I am so glad I did, because it made me curious about the value of my company. The first call I made was to a business broker, Lisa, who valued my business at around $320,000 based on the current SBA banking standards. As a list price, this was not agreeable to me, especially since the business had practically become passive income for me and was growing at a steady rate year after year.

Knowing what I know about negotiation, and with a firm belief in my value and worth, as well as the newly acquired information that I received from that seminar, I told Lisa I'd accept an offer of no less than $500,000. This was my magic number to let my baby go because it would give me a great opportunity to stretch myself in new ways and push myself in new directions.

I had been in quite a routine and not been feeling challenged for a while. I like pushing my boundaries, living life to the fullest, and optimizing my full potential. But I didn't quite feel like I was challenging myself at this point; I was riding the wave that I had built for myself.

My company didn't have any physical assets—no inventory, no office, no equipment. If I sold the company for $500K, it would be cash in my pocket. I figured if life gave me the opportunity to grab a half a million dollars, I would take it as a sign that there was more in store for me.

I had already been thinking about writing this book and inspiring others through public speaking. I became an active participant in assisting in Lisa's pitch. I targeted the companies I knew would find value in acquiring mine and asked Lisa to solicit them. And I strictly told her I was not negotiable on the price.

Lisa was the ideal business broker to work with. She got a lot of interest pretty quickly. But knowing I was not negotiable enabled her to eliminate many prospects. Around a month later, Lisa was approached by an interested party in South Carolina. The prospect already had a family business in the same industry and was impressed and encouraged by my numbers, my P&L statements, and the overall company profitability. He had an office, with expensive employees, while my virtual model could take him into the future.

He offered to pay my asking price, and because there wasn't a bank loan in the mix, we didn't have to contend with any banking scrutiny over the valuation. To me, this was a sign that I was on a path I was supposed to take. The buyer was a great guy, a great family man, a person of such high integrity and a pleasure to do business with—and he valued me and my business greatly.

I accepted the offer.

Before we closed on the sale, I went to the conference where I was to be a guest speaker. To my pleasant surprise, I had absolutely no stage fright and pulled off my presentation without a hitch. What was even more inspiring was looking into the eyes of people in the audience and seeing how what I shared affected them. I saw heads nodding in agreement and smiles all around. It was inspiring and enlightening. I met a version of myself I hadn't met before. After the presentation, people came by the booth to tell me how much my talk resonated.

This was a pivotal moment for me. I overcame such a big fear by getting onstage, and I conquered it. It's not that I wasn't nervous, but I harnessed that nervous energy and stayed rooted in the faith that I was well prepared. I loved the energy boost I received from being onstage, believing in myself and my message, and sharing motivation to inspire others. This proved to me that more of the same could be in my future.

By this point, I was already in escrow on my business sale and the final closing date was just a couple of weeks away. It's amazing to look back at the timing of my very first public speaking opportunity and the unexpected sale of my company.

It was so beautiful and universally harmonious. I knew in my gut it was right.

Your Money, Your Control

I love my grandmother dearly. As I've written before, she's the only family member who was ever truly there for me when I was younger. She and my grandfather did pretty well for themselves; they both earned incomes, lived frugally, and she invested her money wisely yet cautiously. She was also pretty generous with money when it came to members of her family (my grandmother controlled the purse strings). Since we were quite poor when I was growing up, if it weren't for her, I would have never had braces, glasses when I needed them, or new clothes instead of hand-me-downs—and she even helped buy me my first car.

She paid for her kids' and grandkids' college educations, sent a nice check out to every family member for every birthday or any other celebratory occasion, and she would foot the bills to travel and visit with her beloved family members, paying for hotels, family dinners, and the like.

But as I got older and was able to take care of myself, she still wanted to be that source of financial backing for me. I would naturally refuse it because I never wanted a power imbalance to interfere with our relationship. I noticed how those who would accept her generosity would also at times have a bit of resentment toward her, as if they felt subconsciously that her money entitled her to some type of power over them. I paid careful attention to what I saw as a toxic relationship pattern and simply refused to participate. It forced my grandmother to have a level of respect for me that she didn't have with many of the other family members. Our relationship ended up being the closest because it was real, honest, and not based on a power imbalance. No amount of money would have been enough to replace the valuable relationship that I was able to forge with her.

JOURNALING SUGGESTION

What Is Your Relationship with Money?

Take inventory of your personal finances and check in with where you are in relation to meeting your financial goals.

- What are your current financial goals?
- How are you on track toward meeting your financial goals?
- Where could you use some improvement in working toward your financial fitness?
- If you have some financial stress, what do you think you could do to start working toward eliminating it?
- How well do you prioritize saving for your retirement and your own financial needs versus saving for your kids' college funds or giving financially to others?

PART V

The Balance of Caring for Yourself and Caring for Others

Caregiving takes many forms—from helping older, disabled, or sick family members and friends to tending to the needs of a young family. Many of us don't even consider ourselves caregivers and therefore don't recognize the validity or the need to check in with our own needs and states of mind. Denying our roles as caregivers is a slippery slope toward exhaustion, stress, and an inability to balance our lives.

While the formal definition of caregiving often refers to people who give care to elderly or sick/disabled loved ones, I use the term to cover all forms of caregiving and support to anyone who is considered dependent, including:

- The 85 million moms in the United States
- The nearly half (47 percent) of adults in their forties and fifties who have a parent age sixty-five or older and are either raising a young child or financially supporting a grown child (age eighteen or older)
- Those who care for the 41 million Americans age five and older who have special needs

Additionally, according to Family Caregiver Alliance, "About 44 million Americans provide 37 billion hours of unpaid, 'informal' care each year for adult family members and friends with chronic illnesses or conditions. . . . Family caregivers, particularly women, provide over 75% of caregiving support in the United States."[1]

We have all heard flight attendants tell us to "take your oxygen first." That same principle is why I wanted to dedicate several chapters to the relationship between caring for others and self-love. It has been my experience that the more self-love I practiced, the better a caregiver I became; the better a caregiver, the more self-love I experienced.

Chapter 19 is a general discussion of caregiving to ourselves and others. Chapter 20 focuses on one of the areas where it's hardest to reach a balance: parenthood. These chapters will by no means erase your concerns for your aging parents, your wayward teen, or your special needs toddler, but I do hope they will inspire you to find ways to remind yourself that to love others is to love yourself, just as loving yourself is to love others. Remember: Your love is your power, so when you are caring for others, you *must* hold on to some of your love for yourself.

I want to help you spread that love and retain that power to achieve what I call the balance of love. When this balance is achieved, you become less resentful, tired, impatient, obligated, and self-blaming, which is what your loved one deserves in the first place.

The best part is that when we practice self-love, we show others, in particular our children, how to do it for themselves. And *that* is the greatest gift, because it is the key to a happy and fulfilled life. The goal of caregiving is to nurture others and stay connected to the deepest parts of you, and not to forget the responsibility you have to yourself. Finding a balance between giving to others and respecting ourselves is ideal. You don't have to apologize for who you are or how you feel. You are worthy of love. And you are definitely worthy of your own love.

Chapter 19

Self-Care and Caregiving

We can only love others as much as we love ourselves.
—Brené Brown, *The Gifts of Imperfection*

Is it counterintuitive to think you can give care to others—your children, your significant other, your aging parents—and still be full of energy and love for yourself? We all want to provide care and support to those we love and who need us. But too often we get caught in the trap of completely reallocating to others the time, energy, and love that we should also be showing ourselves. Sacrificing yourself, your time, your passions, your peace of mind, and self-care in lieu of others is not synonymous with caregiving. Why do we believe the two are mutually exclusive, that if we dare to care for ourselves, we somehow are not providing adequate care to others?

Why Do You Care for Others?

With millions of Americans failing to recognize themselves as caregivers, we can fall into self-love traps that sabotage our abilities to love ourselves more. There are several reasons, revealed by the following questions, that we put others first and allow our caregiving responsibilities to consume our energy and capacity to fill our own self-love banks:

- Do you feel obligated, shamed by a sibling or friend, or guilted by something you were taught when you were younger? In these ways, you might be caregiving as a way to be validated or find extrinsic acceptance or love.
- Are you so used to saying yes all the time to feed your own disease to please that you find yourself caregiving for almost anyone who asks or expects you to?
- Do you wrap your identity up in caretaking at the expense of defining your own passions, goals, or sense of self?
- Is caring for others a way to fill a void or avoid facing your own difficulties or issues?

This is not to say any of the reasons as to why you provide care are wrong or right, but it's important to identify whether any of these are key motivators. Why? Because if we are not conscious of the reasons we choose to do what we do, these motivators can turn into self-love saboteurs, which I discuss at length in Part II.

This is where we lose our footing. For instance, saying yes is a noble thing to do; however, saying yes 100 percent of the time, foregoing your own time to replenish, is a major self-love saboteur. The goal is to preserve enough good energy for high-level caregiving. Knowing our motivations reminds us to reserve enough love, care, and power for ourselves. This level of self-awareness keeps us in check and balanced, decreases the chance for resentment, and raises awareness of when our balance might be threatened. Any way you look at it, consider whether you are using caregiving as a way to sabotage your duty to love yourself more.

The Sandwich Generation

The term "sandwich generation," coined in 1981 by social worker Dorothy A. Miller, refers to adult children of the elderly who are "sandwiched" between caring for their own children and their aging parents. According to the website A Place for Mom, "Long-term sandwich caregiving is becoming increasingly common as the population ages. Increased life expectancy, coupled with financial insecurity, means many seniors require family care. At the same time, Millennials are having children later than their baby boomer and Generation X parents, leading to more multi-generational households."[1]

Taking care of two generations is not just physically and economically exhausting; it puts caregivers in between an emotional rock and hard place. Caregivers have to make tough choices, which can cause anxiety and guilt of gigantic proportions. It isn't rare that women find themselves having to choose between their child and their parent. A son's football game or being home to sit with a parent who has dementia? A dance recital over a doctor's appointment? Having to forego parent-teacher conferences because an elderly relative fell. College tuition or elder care?

But not all is lost, as the National Caregiving Alliance shared when it said, "Multi-generational caregiving often leads to close-knit families and strong support systems. . . . Children raised in sandwich generation households have the benefit of growing up with both parents and grandparents, while elderly relatives are able to enjoy time with their grandchildren. In multi-generational households, grandparents can help with child care, and later those children can help care for their aging loved ones."[2]

Refilling Your Power Container When Caring for Others

Because caregiving is one of the many ways we expend energy, monitoring the tank gauge of our power container is critical to our self-love journey. Life is a give-and-take, and sometimes caring for others—children, parents, friends, coworkers, relatives—can feel much more like a drainage of our energy. Restoring the balance from take to a give-and-take means managing the stress that comes along with our caregiving roles.

Loss of personal time and privacy, social isolation, constant anxiety, and changes in relationship dynamics are often some of the stressors caregivers find themselves experiencing. Ask any new mom who finds herself suddenly holed up with no adult conversation, or note the confusion of role reversal some women experience when suddenly taking on more of a "parenting" role over an aging or disabled parent. We can see how these factors can insidiously deplete our energy to love ourselves. Dealing with the roots of stress is an act of self-love. To deal with them:

- *Ask for help.* Whether you need to have a discussion with your spouse or parenting partner about redistributing the childcare and household duties or engage with a sibling or other family member about balancing parent care, asking for help is something you owe to yourself. Caregiving is not martyrdom, and if the line between the two is blurred, you might find yourself caregiving for the wrong reasons. The people in your life need you and deserve to be within the care of a person with a full power container. Consider: It is much better to be present with 100 percent of your power container full only some of the time than with it half empty or low all the time. Admitting you are tired, expended, impatient, and need a break is not an act of weakness; it is quite the opposite. Ask for help.

> The people in your life need you and deserve to be within the care of a person with a full power container.

- *Share your feelings.* Many people have found support groups to be a wonderful source of power. Besides providing mutual support, groups can be a source of information and education, as sharing ideas is a big part of community. Mommy classes that allow women to vent, discover they are not alone, and learn self-compassion can also be a great exchange of life hacks, home remedies, and childrearing strategies that help you feel empowered and in control again.

- *Improve your relationship.* Research has shown that the more positive you feel about your relationship with the person receiving care, the less stress you will experience. Don't be afraid to talk about what's on your mind. In doing so you might be allowing the other person an opportunity to talk, which they might have been secretly wishing for themselves. If need be, get counseling, or in the case of a conflict, find a third party to mediate.

- *Get out of your bubble.* Reach out to people, make new friends, initiate conversations. If possible, shake up the routine of you and whomever you are caring for. Yes, it might be annoying to pack up the little one for a ride to the duck pond, but you'll be glad you did. Don't shy away from visitors. They don't have to be a source of stress or require a grand spread of food or energy. In fact, research shows that people who have more frequent, brief visitors report lower stress levels. Again, it's about breaking up the monotony and undoing the feeling that you are living on an island all by yourself—because you're not!

- *Consider care-pooling.* We all know the concept of car-pooling, sharing driving duties of our children, so why not try care-pooling—when several caregivers take turns covering for one another, or chip in for the cost of hiring one attendant. I've seen this become really successful for some moms of young ones. They found a grad student who was majoring in elementary education, who was in need of a job, and they pooled together funds once a week, so the sitter could sit with five of their children while they got their self-care needs taken care of. I personally care-pooled with my neighbor who was the mother of my son's best friend. We were both single moms, so our self-care needs were met by the mutual support we provided one another.

Accept Your Imperfections

One more piece of advice to help you find a balance between self-love and caregiving: Avoid the trap we can fall into of tying your self-value into how well you believe you're providing care. In the next chapter, I talk about how I had to fight against the feeling of failure when my son's life trajectory took a sudden turn. If you are acting in the role of caregiver, you've probably struggled with the same issue.

Overcoming a sense of failure when we feel we've let a loved one down is not easy to do, but it's worth the hard work to get to that place of realizing you are not perfect. To expect you ever will be is not an act of self-love; it is self-punishment. This unrealistic view can leave us always stressed, which depletes our power container and undermines our ability to show up for others in a state of love (or full energy). However, there are some mind shifts we can work on to avoid negative thinking and to refill our power containers. These mind shifts might not come easily and probably will require constant reinforcement, but the following table demonstrates some of the sabotaging self-talk to catch in the moment.

Perceived failure	Sabotaging self-talk	Reality
We fall short against an imagined ideal	"I'm not doing this as well as so-and-so." "How come I don't have my sh*t together like she does?" "I'm not cut out for this." "My parent/child/spouse would be better off with another caregiver."	Comparing and contrasting is not self-love.
We made a mistake	"I screwed up." "I should've been more patient." "Why didn't I do more?" "How could I not see there was a problem?"	Guilt will get you nowhere.
We can't fix a serious issue, such as a life-threatening health issue	"I can make him/her/them better, as long as I try harder/read more/practice more."	We don't have power over debilitating illness. Your presence in their lives is enough.

A little humility goes a long way. Accept your faults. Educate yourself and empower yourself, but don't have unrealistic expectations. You'll preserve energy—the energy you need to do things for yourself like meditate, plan healthy meals and exercise, practice self-compassion, reach out to others for help and support, and partake in positive self-talk and affirmations—so you may remember your own goals, fulfill your own purpose, and take heart in the fact that nowhere does it say because you give care to others, your life is no longer valuable.

Value Yourself, Value Others

Caregiving does not mean your life no longer matters beyond the care you give. Caregiving does not subjugate you to absorb the bad choices, the mistakes, and the consequences a child or other dependent experiences. Caregiving, when balanced, can enhance your life and enrich your relationship with yourself and those you care for. With more and more people being sandwiched between children and aging parents, a society increasingly wrought with mental health issues and addiction, and a generation of adult-age children who are failing to launch because of debt, lack of job opportunities, or a general malaise, I fear that too many women believe, as I once did, that they need to sacrifice themselves to manage the obstacles and challenges of those they love.

JOURNALING SUGGESTION

How to Care for Yourself while Caring for Others

As a caregiver, have you given up some of the things you once loved doing to fulfill what you see as your caregiving duties? If so, list some of what you've given up.

What could you do to start taking better care of yourself and your needs as much as you are taking care of others?

Chapter 20

Losing and Finding Self-Love through Parenthood

When I gave birth to my son, Vincent, I was only twenty years old. I suddenly found myself married, a mom in charge of a helpless infant, and living abroad in the Netherlands. Working in a job I found unfulfilling and not having many friends, I believed the sole reason for doing anything was for the sake of what I thought were my wifely and motherly duties. In just a few months, I fell into a low-energy depression. Confusion and discontent, coupled with fluctuating hormones and lack of sleep, turned me into a shell of the person I was and walled me off from the person I wanted to be. My power container was not only empty; it was rusting and cracking. I didn't have any hobbies of my own, I wasn't practicing any self-care, and my relationship with my husband was tumultuous.

I had mistaken self-abandonment for parenting. Far too many women allow misconceptions of parenting to rule their lives, emptying their power container until they no longer have the energy to love themselves, ironically rendering them less capable caregivers. Blogger Shelly Stasney, MEd, for her blog *This-n-That Parenting*, discussed the misconceptions she had that caused her to lose herself in her role as Mommy. They are so universal that I know I have thought some of these exact same things myself. Shelly said she thought any combination of the following thoughts. Maybe they have been your own as well.

- Doing something just for myself would be selfish.
- Serving my family is my purpose.
- I will pray myself out of this depression.
- My children came later in life. I did plenty of "living" before they came.
- My kids are young. They need me all the time.[1]

Ultimately, my entire outlook on how I would parent was transformed, and, thus, I have avoided many of the typical pitfalls and traps associated with caregiving. In my case, I learned to navigate the unique and delicate period of parenthood when a child is coming of age. I learned (in many cases, the hard way) the importance of remaining individualized and not wrapping my identity and self-worth up in my son, his choices, his successes, his decisions (for better or worse), and his priorities. Having self-love means that even after you bring another beautiful soul into the world and nurse him and mother him, you carry out your duty to ensure you cultivate the gift of your own divinely given life. Self-neglect and self-denial are not adequate tools to care for others. Let me tell you the story.

Your Child's Journey Is Not Yours to Control

Believe me, I am guilty of trying to make my son the person I wanted him to be—instead of shepherding the person he was born to be. I did this through money, judgment, threats, and tough love. I was so consumed with how he was turning out and what kind of reflection that was of me that I lost myself and my sanity. And ironically, the more I imposed my expectations on him, the more I lost a piece of our relationship and bond. It took a tragedy to show me there is a better way.

Vincent was a full-time student at California State University, majoring in film and TV production, which was his passion. He is a talented videographer and editor and was making good money working on freelance video projects for which he'd shoot the footage with his expensive video camera and edit on his fancy MacBook Pro. He was also working as a camera operator for a helicopter company, shooting police car chases and wildfires for local news networks. At just nineteen years old, Vincent was the youngest person the company had ever hired. One time, he sent me a text message to tell me he was in a helicopter shooting footage of wildfires that was being broadcast live on CNN. Quite the proud mom, I tuned in to watch.

His twenty-first birthday was approaching, as was the Coachella music festival. He was excited to go and experience all the live music and to hang out with my boyfriend's older daughter and her friends. I was excited for him.

When he was returning, Vincent rang me. As I answered, I was excited to hear the details of the festival and his experience. But what I got on the other end of the phone did not sound anything like my son. He wasn't coherent, and he rambled as if he were on drugs. I asked him if he had done any drugs while he was there. At first, he claimed he did Molly/Ecstasy. Later he'd tell me he did mushrooms and Ecstasy. At least he *thought* it was Ecstasy. He'd met these guys, total strangers, who gave him a pill, and he took it. This was the first time in his life he had ever confessed to doing any drugs. I promptly called his dad, who lived in LA not too far from Vincent. I asked him to please check in with him and stay in touch with me. I just hoped that everything would be okay once he came down from the drugs.

That never happened.

In fact, things got worse. Over the next few days, he was just a rambling mess. He would go to his classes but then would talk utter nonsense to me on the phone. He was hallucinating and hearing voices. My whole world stopped. I jumped on a flight from Atlanta, where I had just bought a new house the week before, to LA. When I arrived, I remember looking into his eyes and seeing that the light was gone. I didn't recognize him. I was absolutely distraught and beside myself with grief, stress, and anxiety. I didn't understand at all what was happening. I knew had to be strong and responsible and try to help him keep his life together, while at the same time I needed to get him the best medical attention.

My son got very skinny. He stopped taking care of his hygiene, not showering or washing his clothes. He stopped caring about his appearance, stopped doing anything with his hair, and stopped shaving. He had to drop out of school, and he lost his job. It just got worse and worse. I'd Skype with him often, so I had a visual on him. One day, he started making involuntary body movements, like ticks. His head jolted; his arms flinched. Panicked, I called his father and asked him to take him to the emergency room, since I was across the country in Atlanta. He was diagnosed with Tourette's syndrome with psychosis. While this diagnosis was heartbreaking, I felt some relief in that at least we found some answers. And there was hope that perhaps medication would provide some help.

The medications helped stabilize him a bit, but Vincent never returned to normal. He'd enroll in classes at the local community college, only to drop out because he couldn't think straight or focus. Brain scans showed nothing was wrong with his brain or body. Over time, the Tourette's diagnosis couldn't be verified; the involuntary movements stopped shortly after his hospital stay. Unfortunately, though, while still living on his own, Vincent decided to stop taking his medication. During this time off his meds, he announced he wanted to couch surf across the country, which prompted him to let go of his rent-controlled apartment and everything he owned, including his expensive videography equipment and his car. His grandparents, who lived in the Netherlands, intervened and asked if he wanted to come stay with them for a while.

He accepted the offer and went to their house with nothing except his laptop, which, during an unmedicated psychotic state, he punched, leading to its destruction. Absolutely aghast at his behavior and at their wit's end, his grandparents said he needed to return to the US and get back on medication and get stabilized. But now he had no home to return to. He went to stay at his dad's one-bedroom apartment, which didn't last very long.

My boyfriend and I offered to let him stay with us. At this point, Vincent was once again stabilized on medication, so there was some progress on that front. During his time with us, it was apparent that he was capable of getting basic work done. So after a few months, we came to an agreement: Vincent would be welcome to live with us under the condition that he get some type of work, part time or full time, as long as he remained productive.

The deal was that he had to have a job within a few months' time. My boyfriend and I helped him figure out what kinds of jobs he could apply for, helped him write his resume, and tried to build up his confidence. He really wanted to stay with us, and with his limited capabilities, it would seem his only hope for work in his current state would be to work in the food service industry or do some type of factory or manual labor. He would have to learn to accept that this was his new reality, at least under the current circumstances.

My boyfriend, being very family oriented, was kind enough to help him out and drove him to various restaurants and grocery stores around town, waiting while my son filled out applications. He wanted to give Vincent encouragement and motivation, as he thought providing him male support may have a better chance of getting through to him.

A couple of months later, Vincent was offered a part-time job at a frozen custard shop, working behind the counter. The only caveat was that because of the franchise's operating standards for food preparation, he needed to trim his beard to a length of around one inch or less, or shave it altogether. He wanted to instantly refuse the job because he said it had taken him so long to grow his beard out, which was around six to seven inches by that point. To me the beard looked pretty ragged, but longer beards were the current trend with the younger guys at the time. We reminded him that the clock was ticking and that the expiration date on his stay with us was just a couple of weeks away, unless he secured a job.

His choice was clear: Go back to sleeping on the couch at his father's apartment, or shave his beard so he could take the job and stay with us in a welcoming home with his own bedroom. After contemplating it for a couple of days, Vincent opted not to take the job and not to shave the beard. This was the moment where I had to fight the urge to do what I thought a parent should do, which is fight him to shave the beard, tell him how disappointed I was, or give in and extend the deadline. I felt that if I did that, I would be consumed by my son's inability to become a rational adult. I was starting to feel consumed by the notion that somehow I had failed as a mom. But instead, I chose to love myself more. Whether to shave his beard was not my decision, and his not shaving was in no way a measure of my ability as a loving parent. I loved myself enough to draw the line.

So I let his father know of our son's decision and told him Vincent was no longer welcome to stay with us as a result. His father got quite upset with Vincent and told him that as a result of his regretful decision, he would no longer be welcome to stay with him either. So now our son had nowhere to go, and he accepted his fate. He understood that once his plane landed in LA, he would be homeless. I was willing to let this happen and not to intervene, in the hopes that perhaps it would help him change his mindset after hitting rock bottom. But that never came to pass.

Vincent's best friend, who he's known since he was the age of two, asked his mom to pick my son up from the airport and let him crash on their couch. They too lived in a small two-bedroom, one-bath apartment. So that's where my son stayed. And he's been there ever since.

I sent the friend's mother some money each month and asked her not to tell Vincent; I didn't want him to feel unmotivated to take responsibility for himself. But I also didn't want her to have to be responsible for covering his food costs. His dad and grandparents would also give him a bit of money to be able to get by. Eventually he got a part-time job at a coffee shop and earned a little money of his own. He enrolled in community college at least a couple of additional times, both times dropping out before completing any of his classes.

I took this cue from the universe to back off and move into a state of acceptance. I could have chosen to continue to try to take responsibility for his life and his outcome, trying to control things and force them to be as I envisioned them for him. But he and I were on completely different paths in life. And for my own peace of mind, and just peace in general, I had to move all the energy I'd been putting into trying to fix him back into me and my life and focus on my own life's purpose.

It also wasn't doing our relationship any good to be upset with him all the time for making what I considered poor life choices. And it wasn't helping him either. The life I had once hoped he'd have, the opportunities I'd tried to provide him with, all that was gone now. My vision for his future had no bearing on what his life was going to be. His life was his life, his path was his path, and I needed to release that to him.

And so that's what I did. That was more than three and a half years ago as I write this book. Since then, Vincent got approved for monthly disability payments, he's on the California state health insurance that's free for those who don't make much money, and he gets subsidized for groceries. He fully accepts his lot in life. But he realized he needs to make a bit more money to support himself, so he has since taken part-time work at a restaurant. In a bit of luck, his friend's mom got married and moved out, leaving her furnished apartment to Vincent and his friend.

> His life was his life, his path was his path, and I needed to release that to him.

Different lives, different minds, different perspectives. As his mother, I've chosen not to think of his life choices as somehow representing me anymore. The old me would have tried like hell to get him to live a life up to the standards that I had wanted for him, all the while being controlling, imposing guilt on him, and creating unnecessary stress in both of our lives. I now realize that's an ego-based way of looking at my son's life. As I mention in Chapter 5, Deepak Chopra's writing introduced me to the "ego-based" concept. As he is widely quoted as saying, "Make a decision to relinquish the need to control, the need to be approved, and the need to judge. Those are the three things the ego is doing all the time."[2]

When I'm practicing self-love, I would not allow someone else to impose their choices on me, so why would I think my son should accept my choices for him? That kind of external focus of my energy would be a major saboteur of my self-love practice.

I also backed off completely in handling any of his medical affairs. Funny thing is, at some point, he found it in himself to take the initiative regarding his medical care, his medications, and his dental needs. It took me backing off for him to finally develop some kind of concern and agency for his own life and well-being.

Struggles with Paternal Guilt

I accept Vincent for who he is, love him unconditionally, and realize that there is absolutely nothing to feel guilty about. Guilt seems to be this very pesky maternal emotion that can easily control us and keep us from living our best lives as mothers. Somehow over the generations, mothers have allowed our guilt to skew our maternal responsibilities in ways that make us bring up our kids to adulthood and take responsibility for their lives as if they were our own.

I've seen similar scenarios play out with countless mothers of adult children over my lifetime. I recently recounted the stance I took with my son to a friend who also has an adult son with some mental health issues. She'd been feeling incredibly weighed down and a bit hopeless, thinking that caring for her adult child, who despite his issues was still capable, would be her fate for life. And this brought her a lot of stress and anxiety, keeping her energy low and feeling hopeless. He didn't treat her kindly and was verbally abusive to her.

Insight into our guilt mechanism, to the reality that we all have our own fate, gave my friend a renewed sense of empowerment. Her son had other options besides her; she just had to look at those other options and decide for herself the life she wanted to live.

Our children's lives are not *our* lives. And as mothers, we are not destined to live their lives for them or take complete responsibility for them. Poet, writer, and author of *The Prophet* Kahlil Gibran poignantly wrote:

> Your children are not your children.
> They are sons and daughters of Life's longing for itself.
> They come through you but not from you.
> And though they are with you yet they belong not to you.[3]

My son is content. He is safe. He's fed. He is back in school and learning again. He has all the basic necessities in life and more. And our relationship is so much better now. I'm certain he would not prefer to live with me, in a situation where I'd be stressed, miserable, and low on energy all the time. Because that's exactly what would happen. I can't be around the kind of state of mind he lives in without it affecting me negatively, even if it is the energy of my own child. His view of life and my view of life are entirely different. And because I am my highest priority, I have to look out for myself and my happiness first and foremost. I can't worry about what I think others may think of me, thus acting based on that, and then subsequently putting myself in a situation that works to my own detriment.

I don't own my son. He is his own person, his own unique individual, with his own path in life. The best thing I've found I can do for him is to listen, give him unconditional love, not judge him, encourage him—even if it's about the little things in life—and give advice sparingly and only when he asks for it. This behavior actually feels more authentically like caregiving, the kind that is meant to be given, which has brought me peace and has allowed me to continue thriving in my own life, guilt free.

A trap we fall into as parents is to believe we have to mold our children into someone else, someone who they are not. We also believe children are reflections of us, and when we personalize it to that degree, it is a beeline to failure. With lots of tears, the heaviest of hearts, and tons of relapse, I finally was able to remove the propensity of seeing my reflection in my son. Once I did that, I finally was able to succeed in providing him with the level of caregiving he deserved: the kind that did not enable him, showed him complete acceptance and respect, and gave him his right to agency. I think I served him much better than if I had controlled him with my money and power, with guilt or shame, all of which would have been easier for me to do than let him go.

When I told my son I wanted to talk about our journey for a podcast and asked if he would be willing to do this, he enthusiastically agreed. He said he was proud of me and all that I was accomplishing, including writing this book. He also said he doesn't disagree with how I handled our relationship; he believes my letting go and not personalizing his life choices was the best thing for us both.

The Parenting Paradox

The goal of parenting is not to tell our children what to do but to prepare them for independence, to not need to lean on us to make every decision or seek our approval every step of the way. They should not be governed by us, as we should not be governed by them. Yet far too many of us violate this. When I struggle with the guilt that stabs through my protective covering of self-love, I remember the words Marvin G. Knittel, EdD, wrote for *Psychology Today*. I hope they help you as well: "We are the adults who will always be the 'satellite' on which our children's GPS is focused. We will always be there for them. We will empower them but not control them. We will confer with them and always respect their decisions, even when we disagree."[4]

Be a Role Model of Self-Love

I hope you know by now that loving yourself is not selfish. But for some reason, when it comes to our children, that logic goes out the window. If we are to be role models, though, isn't one of the best lessons to teach our little ones to take care of themselves, to value themselves above all others? If you want your children to truly feel self-worth, you need to be a role model by learning how to love yourself first.

"Our ultimate goal in raising our children is to give them the means to know, learn and experience success and happiness; self-love is at the root of those traits," writes Susan Roulusonis Pione in her article "Self Love vs. Parenting: It's Not One or the Other."[5] She points out that children learn first by the example that we set as parents. If we do not show self-love to ourselves, our children will learn that self-love doesn't matter. They will look for external validation on their every action, as I discuss in Chapter 5. To become truly self-reliant, children must practice self-love.

I'll say it again: Loving ourselves is *not* selfish. Because we are making sure we have enough of ourselves to give, self-love is a selfless act. Pione continues, "The only way to teach your children to be happy is to be happy yourself—that starts with self-love."[6]

What's Your View of Parenting?

- How do you currently view your role as a parent?
- Does guilt ever affect your parenting approach? If so, how?
- How could you be a better role model of self-love for your children?

PART VI

Commit to Yourself: How to Ground Yourself in Your Personal Power

The biggest commitment you must
keep is your commitment to yourself.
—**Attributed to Neale Donald Walsch**

I n the first *Sex and the City* movie, world-renowned publicist Samantha
Jones, with her three lifelong fabulous friends in tow, attends an auction in New York City, where one socialite's jewelry is being sold after
her billionaire boyfriend unceremoniously turned her out on the street,
rendering her penniless. Samantha swiftly wrangles her friends around
a glass encasement to gawk at a flower ring made of diamonds. "When
I saw it in the catalogue, I told Smith this flower is the essence of me,
one of a kind, filled with fire," Samantha says with gleaming eyes filled
with promise.

Having moved to Hollywood with her boyfriend, Smith, to be his
full-time publicist as he made his way to A-list celebrity, Samantha was
eager to "spend some of my hard-earned Hollywood money."

Intent on buying this ring for herself, Samantha opens the bid
at $10,000 but is immediately countered by a mysterious woman,

presumably taking instructions from a bidder on the other side of a cell phone.

Frustrated, Samantha engages in a swift bidding war, until the ring sells for $55,000. "I draw the line at fifty," Samantha says to her friend Carrie, who consoles Samantha with a rub of the knee.

Back in LA, Smith surprises Samantha with a special package for their five-year anniversary, explaining he wanted to get her something truly special. Samantha opens the box, and there it is, the flower ring she lost at the auction. She graciously accepts, with one caveat: "This is a ring made of diamonds, not a diamond ring." Although gracious, Samantha's expression lacks something: satisfaction. She wanted to buy the ring for herself, and we viewers get the feeling that to Samantha, the flower ring wasn't a piece of jewelry but a statement of her commitment to herself—a symbol of her accomplishments and personal celebration of her soul. Despite Smith's intentions, the ring had been reduced to just a piece of jewelry. Samantha knew it, and the viewers knew it.

Ultimately, toward the end of the movie, Samantha takes stock of her life and realizes she doesn't quite recognize it. Had she slowly changed herself, or had she altered her life to fit her boyfriend's? She decides to leave him, and when she does, this is what she says to him: "I'm going to say the one thing you aren't supposed to say. I love you . . . but I love me more. I've been in a relationship with myself for forty-nine years, and that's the one I need to work on."[1]

On a recent vacation trip, a similar theme arose for me. I saw a ring that I loved. It called to me, even though my brain answered back that it was too expensive. But I felt I deserved it, that I wanted to spend my love on me, and the ring was a symbol of that. So I bought it. Every time I look at that ring when it's on my finger, I feel so much love and appreciation for myself. I love that I bought it for me. The feeling I got from giving it to myself was so much greater than if someone else had bought it for me.

If the ring had been bought for me by a boyfriend or lover, I might have felt some kind of obligation to that person, and in the event that we stopped seeing each other, I may not ever wear it again. Or if the relationship were to end, and I'd kept the ring, the energy that was behind it wouldn't carry positive weight going forward, and it would be stuck in a drawer.

My ring, the one I bought for me, is for life; it cannot be given back or taken away. That is what true commitment stands for. Commitment to self is the only commitment that endures in this world.

The following chapters are all about creating ways to commit to yourself to affirm your self-love and make self-commitment a healthy part of your self-love lifestyle. In Chapter 21, you'll read about paying attention to your body. Chapter 22 discusses five small steps you can take to direct your thinking patterns toward self-love. Chapter 23 explains how to shape your relationships consciously, and in Chapter 24, you'll learn how to respond rather than react. Chapter 25 discusses forgiveness. Chapter 26 explains how to create a self-love loop, and finally, in Chapter 27, you'll embrace your inner warrior goddess.

Chapter 21

First, Be Still (Pay Attention to Your Body!)

*The key is to be in a state of permanent connectedness
with your inner body—to feel it at all times.*
—Eckhart Tolle, *The Power of Now*

The only way to actually feel our real selves, to own our energy and celebrate our story, is to keep attention in the body. We have to be conscious not to let our minds suck our energy away from us. Our thinking literally creates our reality. We energize the things we think about with our own energy. We have the power to give thoughts weight or not. Take that attention (or energy) away, and—voilà!—whatever you're thinking about no longer exists. That's why my way of thinking has evolved over time to "If you don't give it weight, it doesn't matter"—because it no longer has the weight of your attention.

I came to realize how powerful our attention is. As Deepak Chopra wrote, "Whatever you put your attention on grows stronger in your life. Whatever you take your attention away from will wither, disintegrate, and disappear."[1] It's like when someone calls you out of the blue when you've just been

If you don't give it weight, it doesn't matter—because it no longer has the weight of your attention.

thinking about them. That's the power of your attention. It's the reason why prayers have power. Our energy has power. You are powerful, more powerful than you really know. As acclaimed author Marianne Williamson says, "Our deepest fear is not that we are inadequate. Our deepest fear is that we are powerful beyond measure. It is our light, not our darkness, that most frightens us."[2] You have the power to create your world any way you want it, whether it's consciously done or unconsciously (as most of us operate). Wouldn't you prefer to create a world for yourself based on choosing what you actually want to energize, rather than being reactive, letting your attention be pulled this way and that by constant distractions or appeasing the needs of others?

If you aren't in touch with what your energy feels like, you will always be giving it away, because you won't know the value of what you possess. You won't know your value, your worth, and your power. You want to contain some of your energy and use it for your own power container. When you always keep some of your energy within your body, you empower yourself. Once you get used to the amazing feeling of attuning to your energy, you feel the difference when it's gone.

You can't take notice of anything if you are always fluttering about. We need to be observers of our energy. In a world where we are always connected to devices, where our minds and bodies are racing to the next thing, where we are being distracted or entertained at all hours of the day, observation is a lost art. This is a widespread problem, not just for you but for the world over. Learning contemplation, observing, and listening to regain peace only happens when we start with stillness.

Coming to Terms with Stillness

Have you noticed we might have an allergy to stillness?

Ever wait in a doctor's office for hours or sit in a car waiting for your child's baseball practice to end? Or stand in the pharmacy line, which is increasingly a test of our patience? These are opportunities for stillness but instead we lose our minds—panicking about lost time, hating on the person in front of us who is just there for her thyroid medication, and just feeling antsy, ornery, pissed off. We feel compelled to direct our energy into action rather than stillness.

In my own life, I've had to work hard to readjust my perspective on stillness and learn to see that the times when I felt stuck or trapped were really opportunities for stillness and clarity. When I wasn't capitalizing on the long lines at the grocery checkout, I created new habits that purposely carved out "still time" in my life. And I didn't do it by hitting the meditation mat hard or buying gongs and soliciting expensive yogis. (Although I did discover yoga and it changed my life forever!) Doing too much, for me, is setting myself up for failure. So I started small. I learned to stop for a few minutes here and there during the day when I could, whether at my desk, in my car, standing in line, or just being at home alone and between activities. I'd take ten to fifteen minutes after waking up in the morning or before going to bed at night to just sit in silence and work on quieting my mind and my thinking, focusing all my energy in my body, just feeling my energy.

Of course, there are always days when even I can't talk me off the ledge. But those crazy days are exactly the days when I seek out nature to take the time to be still, feel myself, feel my being, and get in touch with the real me, which is beneath the ramblings of my thoughts. To help you get out of your head, try to listen intently to your breath, focus on the sound of the wind blowing through the trees or the birds chirping. All the while, feel the energy in your body. Studies show that nature has a nurturing effect. Being in nature, sometimes even viewing it from afar, can raise cognition, increase mood, and lower blood pressure.

Tune In to Discomfort in Your Body

What I found incredibly helpful when I first went down this journey of feeling my energy was yoga. Some types of yoga include focusing on breath work and feeling different parts of your body—sending your energy to different parts of your body—not just doing a series of exercises. After practicing this for a while, you start to realize the powerful feeling of the attention of your energy, and you can start to learn how to control it. Pretty soon it becomes easier to recognize when you're giving all your attention to external sources or all that constant thinking in your head. If you're interested in trying this for yourself, you can find an easy-to-follow video tutorial on my website at https://jenna-banks.com/moving-your-energy.

When you stop thinking and move that energy into other parts of your body, you start to feel more alive and connected with your body. Even better, if you can just keep some of that attention in your body at all times, you start to feel like more of the real you. This takes a lot of practice. It probably took me years, but I finally got there. It's made all the difference in the world for my well-being and my connection to myself.

You Are Not Your Thinking

Our shame-based thinking takes up a lot of our energy. It basically traps a ton of energy into an incessant thinking loop, making it seem as though we *are* our thoughts. I certainly used to think I was equal to whatever was happening in my mind. Like Descartes's "I think, therefore I am," I couldn't see the separation.

I can assure you that you are not your thinking. You are the energy that far too often gets trapped in your thinking mind. It is your energy that is the source of your power and your soul, not your thoughts.

When you start to tune in to the energy in your body, which is the real you, you can start to be aware of when you feel discomfort or a general sense of uneasiness. Just like knowing what makes you happy, you have to tune in to any feelings of unhappiness, discomfort, anxiety, and stress. Any feeling other than happiness is a sign that you are on the wrong path for yourself.

I remember during my relationship with my ex-boyfriend Dave, I let a major boundary get crossed and didn't stand up for myself like I should have. Not too long after that incident, I had a terrible feeling of searing anxiety in my chest. It was so heavy, it almost burned. The feeling became so burdensome so quickly, I decided to seek the help of a therapist.

I'm so grateful that I decided to speak to a therapist. She quickly uncovered that the physical sensation was the consequence of my not protecting my power and my boundary. After the session, I talked with my boyfriend about it. After seeing for himself how much his behavior had affected me, we addressed the issue, and the anxiety subsided over the next few days.

I've spoken a lot about how I've learned to tune in to my body for any kind of feeling of discomfort. It is my indication that something isn't right in my life, and that I need to pay attention to it and figure it out. It could be a feeling of depression, anxiety, stress; whatever it is, I no longer let any of those feelings overtake me. I just observe them and bring the power of my attention to them. I remove any judgment I might have about the feeling; I just bring my attention to it and don't attach to any thoughts or emotions. I honor whatever feeling is in my body by giving it attention. I remember I am more than my thoughts, especially the ones of shame. Instead, I focus on being the witness of my thoughts, so I tune in to my energy and remain in my power rather than letting my emotions sap my power from me.

I realize that these feelings are just signaling to me the fact that something is wrong in my life. I aim to feel happy and at peace—not just some of the time but all the time. So if I'm feeling anything other than peace or happiness, I have to pay attention to it and figure out what may be causing it rather than attaching an emotion to it or personalizing it. Since I am in tune with paying attention to the feeling in my body, I am able to make better decisions for my life, faster than ever before.

For example, in new relationships, I used to ignore when I felt a lot of stress, anxiety, or general uneasiness. These are not feelings that

I am used to living with, as I generally feel great. I used to overlook those negative feelings, assuming they were caused by some external factor that I would attach the feeling to, such as stress about a money situation.

> If I'm in a new relationship, the depleted energy is my sign to take space and assess how I'm really feeling about where the relationship is heading.

But I've come to realize that if I'm suddenly experiencing unusual negative feelings, then something else is dulling and depleting my energy. If I'm in a new relationship, the depleted energy is my sign to take space and assess how I'm really feeling about where the relationship is heading and whether it's adding value to my life or taking value away.

JOURNALING SUGGESTION

Paying Attention to Your Body

- Write down how well you feel that you are in tune with the energy in your body.
- What could you start doing today to help you better connect with your own energy?
- Think about the things that you tend to give a lot of your attention to, such as worrying about what someone else thinks of you or maybe trying to get positive attention from someone else. What would happen if you simply removed your attention and energy from doing that?
- Where can you start taking small moments of time for stillness, ceasing all thoughts and placing your attention in your body, throughout your day?

Chapter 22

Five Small Steps with Big Impact

A lot of the ideas I talk about in this book require work—hard emo-tional work—to change the thinking patterns of your current life into the new thinking of a self-loving life. Fortunately, though, there are also some simpler things you can do to help make that switch. Let me talk about five of them, starting with the easiest.

1. Adopt an Emblem

Because any kind of commitment takes conscious reminding and work, the ring that I purchased for myself while on vacation reminds me how important it is to show myself love on a regular basis. Now, I love buy-ing myself little gifts, like flowers on a regular basis, to do just that. On my birthday I bought myself a beautiful, expensive bouquet, and it meant so much to me. It may seem like a small gesture, but it actually makes a big difference. I show myself how much I'm worth to me!

I want you to be inspired to show yourself how much *you* are worth to *you* on a daily basis, and find ways to reinforce your commitment to yourself. Doing so doesn't have to require material things at all, but sometimes an emblem helps. I look at my ring as my emblem of self-love. It reminds me, especially on days when I waver, that I hold myself in high esteem, and when I remember that, I am more likely to choose things that nurture my well-being and serve me well. To quote the Spirit of Water website, "We are blessed with our ability to attain deep understanding from simply looking at symbols. . . . We just know the meanings behind the images. . . . A single viewing of a symbol can transform consciousness, behaviors, understanding, and well being. We are forever changed by the symbols we gaze upon."[1]

Reading this book is in itself a symbol of your commitment to yourself. You are carving out time to read it, to contemplate some of the ideas, to do some internal work. Amazing! Decorating your coffee table with this book could make the book itself your emblem. The cover, the title, the fact that you engaged with it becomes your daily reminder that you are your first priority, so when you leave the house to slay dragons, you know you're committed to yourself, without judgment or shame, to win the day.

Emblems come in many forms. Here are just a few ideas:

- *Body art:* Probably the most widespread expression of self-love and self-commitment is in the form of body art, or tattooing. I have a friend who has a couple of small heart tattoos on her wrist to remind her of her commitment to loving herself first and foremost.
- *Life diploma:* Instead of writing a bucket list, write a list of your accomplishments and have it professionally designed and framed. Display your life diploma on your wall, and affirm yourself each day.
- *Blessing:* Hang a mantra on the wall in your entryway. Each day when you leave the house and enter it, look at it, touch it; remember your worth. (This is particularly helpful on the days you come home feeling beaten up.)
- *Adopt a pet:* I had a friend who, after her husband broke up their marriage and took their cat with him, adopted her own cat, naming him Mio, because, as she said, "He is mine, all mine." Mio

became my friend's reminder that she could take control of a situation that had for too long been managing her. A dog lover and previous pet owner myself, I believe in the power of animal companions—not only in the empirical health benefits but in the spiritual component to such deep connection. When you connect deeply, that bond becomes a symbol and reminder of your worth and how much you add value to your companion's life.

- *Be a pineapple:* I stumbled across this quote a while ago, and it made me think adding some pineapple items around my house are good insignias to have: "Be a pineapple. Stand tall, wear a crown, and be sweet on the inside."

- *Display a power piece:* We tend only to remember the bad things and forget the good we do. This needs to stop. Choose an item or find something from your past that reminds you of a time when you held personal power, felt confident and at ease in your skin, or accomplished something integral to your life. One friend has a letter opener on her desk that reminds her of a time she was promoted; another wears dog tags as a symbol of his bravery in service to our country; another friend bronzed her baby's first pair of shoes and sits them on the side of her computer. Looking at power pieces like these reminds you of who you are; they ground you in your essence and reinstate the self-love you want to capture. Power pieces affirm that you are still that person, worthy of love and celebration.

2. Treat Yourself

This could also be called self-care, but for me, I connect with this concept better as treating myself. What you do to treat yourself will vary from person to person depending on what you enjoy. We talked about the ring purchase I made on my vacation, but you can treat yourself in other pampering ways. Nothing says self-commitment louder than scheduling time to literally commit to yourself in the moment.

I just love the occasional foot massage. I've found that a whole-body massage doesn't make me nearly as happy as a foot massage. So when I feel like I can use a little pampering, I book one. I also know that I love listening to music throughout the day. Music just makes my soul happy. When I find that I've gotten out of the practice of having music on during the day, I'm not nearly as happy. When my mood isn't as good as I know it can be, I think to myself, *What will make me feel better?* Music is that instant feel-good remedy for me.

When I'm in a store buying clothes, I never feel guilty about splurging on what makes me feel good. This also goes along with investing in yourself. When you look good, you feel good, and this only has positive consequences in your life.

Now one does have to be careful to recognize whether shopping is attempting to fill some kind of emotional void. This is not healthy at all. If your shopping takes you out of your financial means, it isn't a treat or a healthy situation.

One can always find ways to get your fashion on in a way that works with your financial fitness. I've found just as much pleasure shopping at TJ Maxx as I have at high-end boutiques, for one-sixth of the cost. And I find it quite rewarding when I can save money at the same time.

3. Stop Saying "I'm Sorry"

For some reason, many women have a natural tendency to want to apologize for everything. You bring yourself down when you say "I'm sorry" all the time. Why are we so sorry? If men were to do this all the time, we'd probably see them as weak, unsure, or inexperienced. So how do you think unnecessary apologizing makes us look?

This issue probably should fall under the chapter on undoing old conditioning, but I felt that it deserved its own focus. By quickly jumping to "Sorry" or "I'm sorry" for every little thing we do, including speaking up at work, we take on a submissive role. Basically, we are telling the world that we are sorry for being ourselves; we are devaluing ourselves. How are others supposed to value us when we are constantly apologizing?

I know at first it might be difficult to stop this. It's like saying, "Fine, how are you?" as a default answer to "Hi, how are you?" It means nothing, yet we say it off the bat. To start retraining your brain and stop apologizing, here are some strategies:

- Make a mental note each time you say "sorry" when you've done nothing wrong. Then stop saying it. Your inner critic will want to judge you for not saying it, but you will be pushing back, committing to yourself and your competence. You'll slowly begin to realize that you don't miss it when you stop saying it. The side effect of not saying it is that you start to build your personal power.
- If there is a need to pardon yourself, try saying "pardon me" or "please excuse me" instead of "I'm sorry." Sorry and pardon are two different things. To say pardon is much more relevant to the situation.
- If someone says something that prompts you to empathize, rather than say, "I'm sorry," consider "So sorry that happened to you."
- If you make a personal error, try saying "oops" instead.
- If you have an idea you'd like to share in the boardroom or want to make an opposing point, instead of opening with the belittling "I'm sorry," say, "I have an idea," or "What do you think about this solution?"

4. Let Go of Perfectionism

On an episode of *Shark Tank*, Barbara Corcoran gave some constructive criticism to a female entrepreneur by telling her that her striving for perfection would hold her back from real success in business. She went on to say that she herself had to learn that 80 percent was good enough, and that belief allowed her to grow her company.

This really hit home for me. Perfectionism holds us back from letting us enjoy our achievements. Perfectionism can also cause us to procrastinate. This is because, according to Brené Brown, best-selling author of *Gifts of Imperfection* and *Dare to Lead*, perfectionism is not the key to success. Rather, research shows that trying to be perfect detracts from achievement and is related to depression, anxiety, addiction, and life paralysis or missing out on opportunities. "The fear of failing, making mistakes, not meeting people's expectations, and being criticized keeps us outside the arena where healthy competition and striving unfolds," says Brown.[2]

When we learn it's okay if something is good enough, we can move on from the task at hand and on to the next thing. It opens up progress on a much faster level. I realized I needed to move from a mindset of having everything be "perfect" to having it be "good enough," or else I would never be as productive as I would like to be. Once I absorbed the concept of "good enough," I was able to grow my business. I focused on nailing 80 percent of what I did, which also kept me from expecting perfection from employees. Now I was able to accept the imperfections of others, which allowed me to let go and hire others so my business could scale, applying the 80 percent rule to their accomplishments.

It's no surprise that people use perfectionism as protection against that icky word—here we go again—shame. When we feel shame, we self-abandon, when what we really need is to remain self-committed. According to Brown, we become addicted to perfectionism because when we finally do experience shame, blame, or judgment, we believe it's because we weren't perfect enough. "Rather than questioning faulty logic of perfectionism," writes Brown, "we become even more entrenched in our quest to look and do everything just right."[3]

When I find myself falling into this trap, this is where "good enough" comes in as a great way to regain my footing.

Brown continues, "Perfectionism actually sets us up to feel shame, judgment, and blame, which then leads to more shame, judgment, and blame: *It's my fault. I'm feeling this way because I'm not good enough.*"[4]

5. Be Kind to Your Body

If you don't take care of your body, where will you live?

—Attributed to Kobi Yamada

Caring for my body affects my energy. There are certain things our bodies need to make us feel good physically and emotionally. Taking care of our bodies is showing love to ourselves. If we are disheveled all the time or don't practice consistent hygiene, we tell the world we've given up on ourselves, we show a lack of commitment to ourselves. We say, "I'm not worth my own time or energy, and you should feel the same way toward me."

How I feel about my body affects my confidence level. When I'm at my desired weight and fitness level, I feel good in my body. It's not about how someone else may perceive me. It's about how good I feel about myself. When I'm happy with my body, I enjoy fashion more, I feel more confident in sexual situations, and I feel more whole as a person.

But caring for your body goes beyond just physical weight and appearance. It's also how you treat it on the inside. I know that after too much drinking, I basically waste almost the entire next day recovering. Depending on how much I drank the night before, I can feel anxious the next day, lethargic, and am very unproductive. I also eat terribly when there is alcohol involved. If I do that too often, I begin to feel badly about myself in general and then begin a cycle of feeling just icky. And it can turn into a vicious cycle.

Drinking makes you feel like you don't have a care in the world—for the moment, anyway. But then the next day, you look in the mirror and get upset with yourself for not resisting the temptation. I found that when I can break the cycle for a few days, I can then start feeling proud of myself for being good to my body. I take a moment to recognize that I made better choices the last few days and assess and recognize how good I feel. My skin looks considerably healthier, I get better sleep, and I have more energy for exercise. I also make a mental note that this good feeling lasts all day and is something that I prefer over the temporary moment of enjoyment that may come from drinking too much.

The same goes for eating. Our bodies function at a much more optimum level when we eat whole foods and eliminate foods that cause us problems. My general rule is to try to avoid processed foods and food that would take longer than a week to expire—to become inedible—after sitting in the cupboard or refrigerator. It's not that I don't allow myself to eat cookies, crackers, or other packaged food from time to time, but they are not a normal part of my diet and I eat them in moderation.

I found that diets don't work for me. If I feel like I am not allowed to have something, it'll make me want it even more. I can have it if I want, but if I think about how I'll feel afterward or how much it may take me off track from my optimum body weight, this mindset helps me make better choices.

I now actually crave eating healthy foods. I feel like my brain has rewired itself to seek out natural, healthy foods. I get excited when I see a beautiful salad full of greens and multicolored veggies. My body knows it's going to feel good after eating them.

Now in the grocery store when I pass by the ice cream section, what used to be old temptation and automatic craving response is replaced by knowing that how good I feel is more important than how good it tastes. Basically, sugar was an addiction that I got over by getting out of the habit of eating it. That addiction was replaced with the addiction of the good feeling I get when I eat healthy, whole foods.

I do, however, want to offer a caveat: Taking care of our bodies does not mean we should neglect our emotional needs when it comes to our bodies. As women, so many of us spend much of our lives rejecting our bodies for what they aren't. This became apparent to me when I was having a conversation with a friend of mine recently. She currently weighs around twenty pounds more than she weighed a few years ago—but that was a time when she was doing a lot of physical labor. Her reduced weight was unsustainable in the real world. But to her, that "twenty pounds lighter" is her "ideal weight."

While my friend has occasionally been at the "twenty pounds lighter" weight in the past, mostly her weight has been over her ideal weight. And because she's not close to her ideal weight, she's frequently putting her body down and living in a mode of self-rejection. Recently she was having yet another one of these self-rejection conversations with me, and it hit me that not only is she *not* showing herself love, but she's treating herself in a way that we'd never think was okay for anyone else to be toward us (especially a boyfriend, lover, or friend) simply because of our weight difference.

When I realized this, it made me sad for her. Then I realized that I do exactly the same thing. I beat myself up when I put on weight and talk and feel negatively about my body. From conversations I've had, I think many women fall into this pattern. Somehow, we believe that beating ourselves up is good for us. But it doesn't really work like that. Beating ourselves up isn't a good motivator at all, will never lead to weight loss, and really works against our self-love game too. Just thinking of all the negative energy we send to our bodies on a regular basis is really heartbreaking.

Since that realization, I've made a conscious effort to stop beating myself up for weight gain. These times of weight gain are times when I need to be kind to myself and forgive myself for getting off track from my usual eating and exercising habits.

Life happens. And just like we'd expect our partner not to hold weight gain (or loss) against us and love us less for our body weight, we should be giving ourselves that same loving-kindness and acceptance no matter what. We need to love ourselves both inside and out, and this includes our bodies.

So every time my extra weight crosses my mind, I forgive myself and find ways to love my body. I've found it's really not difficult to make the change in my approach. I just needed to be conscious about what I was doing to myself and then make a conscious choice to choose a more loving way to treat myself. And really, how can we expect anyone else to love our bodies at any weight if we don't even love it ourselves?

Now that I've taken on this approach to my body, I realize it hasn't changed my motivation to still aim to be at my ideal weight when I get off track. But when I do get off track, I don't feel bad about myself anymore.

Practicing with Small Steps

My goal in this chapter was to provide enough simple suggestions so that anyone reading this book would find at least one they could say yes to. What do you think will work for you? Do you have or could you buy or create an emblem to symbolize your commitment to yourself? Is there something you could do today to treat yourself because *you* think you are worthy of your appreciation? Do you think for one day you could remove "sorry" from your vocabulary except for when you were at fault? Are you a perfectionist who might be able to try what it's like living with "good enough"? Can you do one new thing today to take care of your health?

As you no doubt realize, there are some changes associated with learning to love yourself more that are not easy and may take a long time to master. But I'm hoping these ideas will help you make progress quickly in a few areas—and inject some fun into the equation as well!

JOURNALING SUGGESTION

Treating Yourself Better

- When is the last time you treated yourself? What can you do to treat yourself this week?
- What do you currently believe about perfectionism? Where do you think that belief came from?
- What kind of self-talk do you give yourself about your body? Do you give your body your love or negative energy?

Chapter 23

Shape Your Relationships Consciously

When we commit to ourselves, we must be aware of the significant others we also commit to. This has a lot to do with boundary setting, but it goes much deeper. Choosing a relationship partner is one of the most important decisions we can make, but we tend to do so with blinders on. Whether we are drugged by an intense chemical attraction, find something familiar and safe about a person, or are driven by a partner ticking all the "right boxes," we need to try harder to be more conscious of who we commit to. We need to be aware of not only who these people are and why we are drawn to them but whether they are aligned with the values we hold high in our lives.

I remember a time shortly after breaking up with Dave. I was hurting so badly. I decided that I needed more advice and guidance than I could give myself. I wanted to get a better understanding of how things went so wrong in the first place. So I went online looking for answers and landed on an article written by someone at a relationship coaching site called Relationship Hero.

I'd gone through traditional therapy after a previous breakup, and that did help me better understand that particular relationship, what drew me to it, and why it eventually fizzled out. But relationship coaching was a very different experience because the coach focuses specifically on how you act and interact when you are in a relationship with some-one else. Coaches use tools more specific to coaching versus therapy, such as uncovering limiting beliefs. Using the onboarding worksheets that Relationship Hero sent me, I was able to immediately see that I had abandonment issues, mistrust, and self-sacrificing issues that I was not even aware of. I also learned that I needed to allow myself to be more vulnerable in relationships.

With my coach's help, I was able to discover that I had been uncon-sciously falling into familiar patterns in relationships, choosing people who were controlling and who allowed me not to have to be vulnerable, which would then feel "safe." But what I felt was "safe" or "familiar" would also trigger all my survival patterns, including having to be strong in a relationship. When I was strong, I felt safe, because that was a pattern that I knew.

I also learned what my "relationship values" were as well as how to spot green flags (the ones that told me I should proceed in the rela-tionship) and red flags that would give me cues as to whether someone actually exhibited the values that I held high.

I had mistakenly thought that when I had chemistry with someone, and they seemed like a decent enough person, that would be enough to give them a chance. Just because you have chemistry with someone, that doesn't make them right for you. In fact, what you think is chemistry might just be the comfort you're feeling from old patterns that present themselves. With the help of my rela-tionship coach, I went through and identified my values, my relationship values, and what I needed from my partner to fulfill my values.

> Just because you have chemistry with someone, that doesn't make them right for you.

It became clear to me that my last partner possessed almost none of the key relationship values that I really needed. Moving forward, it was my job and responsibility to ensure I chose my relationships consciously. Not based on chemistry or attractiveness alone. Not even on love alone. Yes, love is important, and so is connection, and we build on both in our relationships, but this makes me think of that song by Patty Smyth and Don Henley, "Sometimes Love Just Ain't Enough." I know this to be true, especially in my relationship with Dave.

Three Questions for Choosing a Partner

When it comes to choosing our intimate partners, Tony Robbins suggests that we ask three questions, none of which have to do with love or attraction:[1]

1. *"Can they do the job?"* A friend of mine once dated a guy ten years her junior. And while they had passionate sex and unbelievable fun together, she knew she wanted to get married and have children within the next two or three years. Certainly at his age (twenty-four) he was not capable financially or emotionally to enter an engagement. While my friend felt something for this guy and was having the time of her life—and sensed he was falling in love with her too—she decided he couldn't do the job, not the one she was readying to do herself, so she broke it off.

2. *"Will they do the job well long term?"* In business, you are aware that job candidates sell themselves hard and well in the interview process, but, Robbins asks, are their goals aligned with the job? In the case of my friend with the younger boyfriend, maybe he was up for the job of being a committed partner and father, but what Robbins is suggesting is to think about the long term. Would he be capable of sticking around? Of helping her support their family? Would there be any repercussions if he wasn't genuinely and 100 percent committed to the plan? Of course, nobody has a crystal ball, but I see the value in asking this question.

3. *"Is this the right team fit?"* Robbins does a lot of work helping employers bring on new hires who will not just be able to do the job but *stay* with the job because their personal goals and aspirations are a good fit with those of the organization. He suggests doing the same when considering a relationship partner. If both you and your partner list your needs in priority order and your top two needs are the other person's bottom two needs, then Robbins doubts whether you two as a couple will remain happy. This "team fit" concept was something I worked hard on when it came to figuring out what my relationship values were. Now I know to check in with myself along the way, especially in brand-new relationships, and make sure that I'm being true to myself, my needs, and my relationship values. If something is feeling off at any point, I have to be aware of it and address it right away. (I speak more about communicating needs in the next section.)

I now value my time and energy so much. If I'm going to let someone into my space, which I place a high value on, I now have the tools I need to consciously choose a person who actually meets my relationship values.

Core Values

Possessing similar core beliefs is critical if you want your significant other and you to feel connected, protected, safe, and gratified. Some examples of relationship values include, but are definitely not limited to:

- ambition
- familial care

- intimacy
- generosity
- fitness
- communication
- skillfulness
- prosperity
- dependability
- self-discipline
- affection
- sensitivity
- loyalty
- honesty
- forgiveness
- empathy
- intelligence
- gratitude
- orderliness
- authenticity
- sophistication
- moderation
- emotional health
- honor
- devotion
- optimism
- courage

Communicate Your Needs

Many of us are too afraid to speak up and tell someone what we need from them. In fact, I have found that a fear of communicating one's needs is one of the main reasons that women fake orgasms. When women do this, they do not give their partner the opportunity to do their part. They're trying to make their partner feel good at the sacrifice of themselves!

I've always been a great communicator about my needs in relationships. And in every relationship, my partners have always appreciated this about me. Almost every time I brought up my needs, the other party was grateful for getting the opportunity to know what it was that I needed, and I got more of my needs met. They got an exact roadmap from me to ensure that they have an opportunity to know how I'm feeling, at the moment, rather than being blindsided by negative emotions down the road when my silent needs aren't being met.

I've found it especially important to communicate any feelings I may have, right at the time of incident. This gives my partner the chance to understand me when the situation is fresh, rather than having no clue if there's an issue and then having it come out much later down the road after the incident has long past.

"'What will they think of me?' must be put aside for bliss," says Joseph Campbell.[2] When you don't communicate your needs, you are sending the message that what you need doesn't matter. That is the opposite of self-commitment.

It feels good to communicate your needs. If you're not used to doing it, it may be a bit scary at first, especially if you are a people pleaser or worry how the other person might interpret you speaking your mind. But once you face that fear and realize how healthy and good it is for both parties, you'll no longer let that fear stop you.

Take Space to Be Alone When You Need It

When you're living with someone, or you're simply around someone all the time, it can be very tough to have a clear and objective opinion about exactly how you feel about the relationship. When there is an underlying feeling of discomfort about the relationship or you're feeling a bit unsettled with your partner and can't quite put your finger on it, taking space to sort your feelings out is one of the best ways I've found to get in touch with the deepest part of me. This was another lesson I had to learn from experience.

My longest relationship was with a man named Jerry who was more than a decade older than me. When I met Jerry, I had recently moved and was ready to spread my wings.

Jerry was a family man, seemed very stable and secure, and had an attractive, gregarious smile that made you feel like everything was going to be okay. I'd been so independent all my life, and so having a man make me feel like everything was going to be okay was something I suppose I needed at the time.

While I was attracted to him and had love for him, there was always some hesitation with me. His controlling behavior, as well as his lack of financial fitness, were a bit off-putting. I also felt like he pretended that he was very important. He had an inflated ego that was always a bit annoying to me—a complete lack of self-awareness really. He also hid his financial situations from me, which made it a bit concerning when I considered our long-term potential together. But I chose to overlook those issues at first, as he also was very nice to me, showed me love and attention, and was a very stable person.

Since I had just moved, I was mostly living off my savings while trying to ramp up a new business. He was also an entrepreneur working from home like I was. We got pretty hot and heavy, and soon he asked me to move in with him. After my initial hesitation, I agreed. I had been used to being super independent but was willing to take the risk and give this relationship a go. (Side note: I insisted that I contribute to his mortgage to ensure that just because I was living in his house, there wouldn't be an underlying power imbalance between us.)

Since we hadn't been together for very long before I moved in, I got to know him a lot better while living with him. I also got more acquainted with my underlying sense that things weren't exactly where I wanted them to be. I wasn't feeling my usual happy-go-lucky self. My energy always felt a bit zapped, unlike when I used to live alone. I noticed that I no longer liked what I saw of myself when I looked in the mirror. And when I'd interact with strangers, even the cashier at the grocery store, I just felt like I wanted to hide.

One spring we went on an exotic vacation. He had been under a lot of stress with his business venture and had been acting a bit erratically. His small executive team, all of whom were old friends of his, started turning on him and were trying to oust him as CEO of his own company. (Regardless of the reasons he was giving me for his turncoat friends, I had doubts in my head about his version of events. Why would his old friends turn on him without reason?)

While on vacation, Jerry dropped the bomb that we needed to rent out his house—where we both lived—for financial reasons. He said the plan was to move into a tiny rental unit he owned that was in desperate need of renovation. I was in shock. The shock came from the fact that here he was not giving me the respect as a partner that I had been previously concerned about. If he had respected me as a partner, he wouldn't assume I'd be okay with this and just tag along with him wherever his life led him. And he had been hiding his financial situation from me. The only reason why he was telling me now was that he was broke! He had put all his investment eggs into this one basket, a terrible financial decision for someone his age.

I was definitely not okay with living in the small apartment. I'd worked far too hard and done well enough in life that I didn't have to live like that. And now I knew his real situation, the one he'd been hiding from me. I had already had major trepidation about where our relationship was going, and how I'd been feeling overall. I decided I needed to get away and have some space. I still owned two Airbnb rental properties on the East Coast, so I booked a two-week stay at one of them to take some space and spend time with my friends.

I told Jerry not to call me or text me, that I needed space to think about things and to think about this situation he was in. I probably should have followed the advice of Dr. Wagner (as noted on the following pages) and used more diplomacy in my phrasing, but he agreed anyway. Soon after, he began to make me feel guilty about it, like I owed him something. He said that he was going through a tough time in his life and how dare I need space when he was the one "going through" something. Nonetheless, I didn't let him shame me; nor did I let him control my decision, which he tried very hard to do.

My time alone allowed me to think much more clearly. I talked things through with my friends and had time to contemplate in peace, without Jerry trying to influence my decision. I was able to finally feel my energy again for the first time in quite a while. I felt a beautiful sense of peace and clarity.

The more I thought about his situation and how his life choices were negatively affecting my life, the more I realized I was not responsible for him. I also knew that his life path was not what I wanted as my life path. His story was not mine. I had a different vision for my life but found myself only living his.

Making Space for You

The soul needs more space than the body.

—Attributed to Axel Munthe

It may be uncomfortable for you to bring up the old "I need some space" request to your partner. It also may cause a bit of a backlash from your partner if they feel threatened in any way. But the truth is, if they are not willing to give you the space you need to figure out your feelings, they are either being controlling, insecure, or something else (envious maybe?), which has nothing to do with you doing what's best for you.

If your partner really loves you, they will allow you the freedom to be who you are. The truth is, if you come back to them having worked out your feelings and thoughts about the relationship, you'll be in a much better place. But if you have uncovered that you are in a relationship that isn't meeting your needs and isn't fulfilling to you as a person, then it's better to have discovered this sooner rather than later.

It's easy to get caught up in a rhythm with your partner and simply not to want to rock the boat. But going with what you know simply because of fear of the unknown isn't living a life that is fulfilling your needs, and it isn't allowing you to create the story of your life as you really want it to be. It isn't indicative of self-love.

Taking Space Need Not Be a Federal Case

The adage "It's not what you say; it's how you say it" is 100 percent true in the case of explaining to a loved one that you need space. If you are mindful of how you phrase the request, you might find pushback diminished significantly or eradicated all together. Marriage and family therapist Talia Wagner advises that framing your request the right way makes the difference between resistance and your loved one supporting your needs and even planning to use the time for their own introspection and growth.

"If you ask nicely and kindly and stress that it's something you both need and would benefit from, it goes a long way," Wagner told *HuffPost*. "When you deliver this news in an accusatory or frustrating tone, the message is rarely received."[3]

So instead of saying, "I'm feeling overextended and completely burned out between work and the kids and everything in between," which might cause a fight because likely your loved one feels similarly, try to emphasize that your partner could benefit too. So you could say something like, "I think we could both benefit from taking a little time for ourselves."

When you take space for yourself, you might find it helpful to talk to your friends or family members about how you are feeling. Sometimes we can find more clarity when talking to others who are close to us.

Use your private time to observe how you are feeling—emotionally and physically. Do you feel better when you are in control of your space? Do you say things like, "I haven't slept that well in weeks" or "I can't remember the last time I laughed so hard?" Are people complimenting your smile or your demeanor? Do you not crave alcohol or comfort food the way you might have before you took your space? Do you start to see your partner in a different light? If you start to feel your energy lifting and have a better outlook than you've had in a long time, that's a sign that you've lost way too much of yourself in that relationship. Don't forget this personal work is applicable across all different relationships, from your roommate to your boss to your mother.

After you've taken as much time as you need, or as much time as you're able to, and you're still not sure what is best for you, try going back to your situation. But this time, do it in a state where you try to be present in every moment rather than falling into unconscious old behavior patterns. When you go back to your situation, try not to judge anything your partner does as good or bad. Don't attach, react, or personalize. Just observe, ask questions, and let them answer from their truth. Try doing this without getting upset at them, making them feel guilty, or judging them. What you say can color what they say. You want to objectively observe what you are getting from them. Be the witness. If they ask what you are doing, you can simply say you are taking some time to reevaluate where you are in life and are reflecting on the relationship.

The goal is to be objective and not react. Just witness. What is their behavior? Are they showing you love? Are they being controlling? Are they evading the question or turning it back on you? Are they pulling away? Are they trying to infuse fear or doubt in you or make you feel guilty or ashamed for loving yourself more? What is their body language telling you? Are they puffing out, trying to make themselves larger? Are they cowering away in apathy?

Once you observe what they are doing, continue asking questions and continue accepting those answers. Keep asking more questions until you feel you are able to see the truth of "what is" and who this person really is, what their motivations are, how their lens has been formed. Ultimately, if you want love, intimacy, understanding, or any other relationship values that are important to you, you have to decide that you aren't going to accept less for yourself. The bottom line is, not every relationship that we get into is supposed to last forever. Some relationships simply have an expiration date. And that's okay.

Balancing Love for Self with Love for a Partner

In an earlier chapter, I talked about how difficult it is to find a balance between caregiving for ourselves and caregiving for others. The same is true in dealing with romantic relationships. You want to be in love. You want to give of yourself to support your partner. But you can't give away so much of yourself that you have nothing left to nurture your own hopes and dreams.

That's why in this chapter I'm encouraging all of us—myself included—to be more conscious about decisions we make to bring people into our lives, about what kind of partner we can commit to without endangering our commitment to ourselves. Don't be afraid to speak up for what you want and need from the relationship in ways both large and small. Finding balance is a way to have more fulfilling relationships that will allow you to have more to give both yourself and your partner.

Your Core Values

- Are you aware of your core relationship values? Write down what they are. Use some of the examples given earlier in this chapter if you would find that helpful.
- How well have your previous partners, or current partner, met your core relationship values?
- How well (or not) do you think you currently communicate your needs to those you are in a relationship with?
- How do you feel about taking space when you need it? Do you worry that you might hurt your partner's feelings and thus sacrifice your own needs for theirs? What do you feel would happen if you prioritized your needs over your partner's needs?

Chapter 24

Learn to Respond Instead of React

In the previous chapter, I tell you about Jerry, the older man I dated for a number of years. While we had a good run, I chose to leave because his life choices were not aligned with mine. I felt I had given away too much of myself and my energy was sucked dry. Before I broke up with Jerry and after I took some alone time away from him, I returned to his house to see if we could figure out a way to work it out. But what transpired is an example of what happens when a person does not respond but instead reacts without thought or concern about consequences.

Jerry had been drinking more than ever, and he behaved badly when he drank too much. Here we were supposed to be trying to see if we could salvage our relationship, and he was just digging our grave even deeper by numbing himself with alcohol, a reactive solution in itself. I remember that in one discussion, I told him that I was concerned that he'd put all his savings into his struggling company, especially when he had no emergency fund or retirement savings.

He retorted, ranting about how much more his ex made than I did and went on about several other unrelated things, playing tit-for-tat, which to me is not based in reason at all. The more he reacted like this, the less I wanted to try.

A day or two later, I was reading on the couch. He probably had drunk an entire bottle of wine by himself during dinner within less than an hour. I chose not to have any wine that evening. He passed by me and said he was headed outside to clean up the yard. I didn't respond, as he liked to think out loud all the time, and I didn't feel like what he said warranted a response.

Next thing I knew, he came raging back into the house, calling me a bitch because I didn't acknowledge what he had said. I'd never seen this side of him before. Besides calling me names, he started yelling in my face. Both were things he'd never done before. I got scared, as I felt like he might even attack me.

I feared for my safety, so I tried to just keep to myself on the couch and book a plane ticket out of there. He continued screaming in my face, so I moved myself to a bedroom and closed the door. It was important for me to stay calm and not fire back. Believe me, when you are fearful, it is even harder to fight that instinct to flee, to not let your adrenaline take over and inhibit a proper response. But I wanted to respond rather than to react. I knew that reacting would only make things much worse. He forced his way into the bedroom, still yelling nonsensically, making me feel extremely unsafe. So I called the police.

I'd never experienced anything like this before in my life. And especially not from Jerry after all the years I spent with him. When the police arrived, he proceeded to tell them that I didn't live in this house (even though all my personal belongings were there) and that I had to leave his home immediately. My dog and I headed for a nearby hotel. As I was driving there, he was texting me telling me that he was blocking me. Besides the shock of the situation, I also felt a bit of a sense of relief that there was finally going to be a resolution to this relationship. I also felt that once again this was the universe giving me that not-so-subtle shove out the door, letting me know that this relationship had run its course and it was time to move on.

The next day he completely changed his tune. It's amazing what happens when time passes and you have the space to actually process the situation (and sober up). He pleaded with me to come back and stay at the house and even sleep in the guest room. He said he understood that we were done but that I should at least spend the remaining few days at the house before my flight. This was a rational response. But I remained at a nearby hotel. Over the next few days, Jerry was nice to me, as he usually was, and helped me pack up boxes to be shipped to my place out East. He insisted on driving me to the airport, where we said our goodbyes. I left knowing I'd never come back. His reactions showed me the sides of him that made me sure I'd never be able to look at him in the same way again. A couple of weeks after I left, when he could sense that he probably lost me for good, he broke down crying over the phone like I'd never heard a man cry before. He confessed that his behavior that night was one of the biggest regrets of his life. Of course, I felt bad for him that he was in pain. But I didn't let that affect my own decision for my life for one single moment. A few days later, after drinking one evening, he was back to acting terrible again. I cut communication off permanently, made a clean break, and never looked back.

If you want to live a life that you love, you need to love the choices that you make. Most of us are not aware of how many unconscious choices we make in our daily lives that we wind up regretting. We react and then make choices in the heat of those reactions, when we should be learning to respond more thoughtfully. As Ravi V. Melwani is believed to have noted, "The wise respond. The foolish react. The wise think and then act. The foolish act and then regret."

> If you want to live a life that you love, you need to love the choices that you make.

Choosing to Respond Rather Than React

Let's say you drive to work and someone cuts you off. You can choose to allow that situation to upset you, or you can choose not to let it upset you. It really is a choice. I choose to live my life feeling as good as possible throughout the day. And I also choose not to let someone else's behavior get in the way of my happiness. I choose to focus on responding to situations rather than reacting to them, as summarized in the following table.

Reaction	Response
Fear-based	Thoughtful
Defensive	Reasonable
Emotions are in control	Observes emotions
Without reason	Able to influence outcomes
Instinctual, from the subconscious mind	Controls the situation
Short-term view	Long-term view

Just as I knew with Jerry, being reactionary to someone else's behavior puts the other person in control of your energy. You let that person govern your agency. This governance can lead to emotional manipulation, which can make you behave in ways you might not normally behave, reacting to their emotions. But since you are the one engaging and reacting, you can't help but think that your reactions are you.

Nearly every day I encounter people trying to make me feel a certain way by getting me to react, whether to get themselves on my good side with a compliment or to get me to engage in their toxic way of thinking with some kind of negative talk.

Thankfully, I'm so aware of what emotion another person is attempting to elicit, I'm able to choose how I engage rather than react right away based on whatever emotion pops up. That emotion is not me, as it is not coming from a conscious place. Responding and not reacting takes mindfulness and thought and consideration. When you need to respond, you can do so from a sense of strength and confidence, which helps you keep your commitment to yourself and to the way you want to live your life.

To shed light on the difference between reaction and response, certified executive coach Melissa Eisler uses the analogy of a puppy. On her website, Eisler writes, "Reactions are like [an untrained] puppy who . . . bark[s] at every dog it sees, jump[s] at every passing neighbor, and then . . . eat[s] your dinner. . . . Responses are more like the well-trained . . . dog who comes when you call him, barks only when there's a reason to bark, and waits patiently for his treat."[1]

Taking the Reins

It takes mindfulness training and lots of practice, but if you can get into the habit of not reacting right away (even just to pause and breathe for a second) to an emotionally charged situation, you will be in a position of being true to your nature. In the space we create in that pause before we react to a trigger, we can observe not just the trigger but also our initial reaction to it. *Why am I feeling this way? Why do I want to hurt this person back? What is it about what she just said that puts me on the defensive? Am I afraid? Do I think she is right? What am I afraid of? If she is right, why does this bother me in this way?* Taking the reins back by engaging with yourself in the moment instead of lashing out puts you in a position of being in your power so you can remain committed to that power.

I talk in the last chapter about taking space. We all deserve space to protect our boundaries but also to figure things out and grow from them. The next time you feel you are about to react instead of respond, Eisler advises creating that space. "Adding that pause—that layer of observation, space, mindfulness, or whatever you want to call it—to the moment when you notice you're triggered can mean the difference between strengthening or breaking a relationship, between a child, lover, colleague, employee, or neighbor walking away feeling supported or disregarded," she writes. "That space could mean a few deep breaths as you allow the reaction to fade and invite your balance to return. Or, it could mean taking a day or a week to cool down and reduce the charge of your emotional response. Every person and every situation will require a different way of doing this. Taking some space when you're triggered gives you the time to make a conscious decision on your next step."[2]

Chapter 25

Forgive

To forgive is not just to be altruistic, it is the best form
of self-interest.
—Archbishop Desmond Tutu, *No Future without Forgiveness*

I've had to grapple with forgiveness many times in my life: with my father, my mother, my ex-husband, my own son. Being raised in a faith where you are taught God forgives you only if you do penance made it more difficult to forgive the people closest in my life for hurting and neglecting me. For a long time, I mistakenly thought forgiveness freed them from their acts, which is not true at all.

Many people confuse forgiveness with absolution. Fred Luskin, PhD, a specialist in forgiveness, was interviewed by Michele Matrisciani for her book *Whole.* He said, "You forgive so you are not captured by a piece of your life. Your brain's real estate is taken up by a very, very bad parent. You forgive so your parent occupies less of your brain as your life moves forward."[1]

Letting Go of Negativity

In previous chapters, I talk a lot about self-compassion and self-forgiveness, but what about letting go of the grudges we hold against others?

When our attention is being given away to others, especially in the form of negative energy, that becomes energy that we don't retain for commitment to ourselves. There is no focus on us, other than ruminating over our victimhood.

If we are capable of forgiving and letting go of resentment and grudges, there will be more room in our hearts for compassion and love. Holding on to grudges only hurts us in the end, not the other way around. Why would anyone consciously want to continuously hurt themselves?

I remember when I was in my early twenties, I was in a sales position and a female work colleague stole a potential high-ticket prospective client from me. She was somewhat new to sales, and what she did went against the rules most trained salespeople know to follow. When I complained to my other colleagues and manager, they all said she should get a hall pass since she was new, not to mention that they were all men and she was a blond bombshell. Though she and I had become quite friendly before that, she knew I was very upset, hurt, and angry about the situation. I remember that I held on to that anger for many days—it might have even been weeks.

Then one day it hit me: The only person suffering with this anger and resentment was me. My colleague seemed to be going about her life without a care in the world. So why was I causing myself so much disruption in my life?

Forgiving another person doesn't mean the act wasn't wrong, that it doesn't hurt, or that it is forgotten. But it was my choice how I wanted to feel about the situation, how much I would allow it to control me, because when you can't forgive, you are not in control.

Dr. Luskin wrote in his book *Forgive for Good: A Proven Prescription for Health and Happiness* that holding a grudge is hazardous to our health. Dr. Luskin has been directing research on forgiveness at Stanford University and has proven the power forgiveness has on the mind, body, and soul. He says forgiveness has been shown to reduce depression, increase hopefulness, decrease anger, improve spiritual connection, increase emotional self-confidence, and help heal relationships.[2]

Forgiveness Can Remove Excuses!

Many people don't forgive so that they can make excuses for not living a full life. "When you don't want to heal, you need an enemy, you need an excuse," said Dr. Luskin. "Let's just say you are a crabby person. It's so easy to say, 'Well, I'm crabby because my father ruined my life.' Or else you will be stuck doing the work that you need to do to stop being a crabby person. Once typical grief runs its course (maybe over a few years), all you have left is your life. You have to figure out how you want to live it most successfully. It doesn't matter what happened."[3]

Once I admitted to myself that I felt like crap over this internal battle I was having with my colleague, I realized that holding on to anger and resentment was something I was choosing. But the ongoing anger and resentment was affecting only me and my energy in a negative way, not the other person. Why would I consciously bring that energy into my life by holding on to a grudge like that?

I decided that I needed to let the negativity go. And the way to do that was to find forgiveness. There's always more than one way to look at a situation. I decided to try to look at the situation from the other person's point of view. Perhaps she didn't intend to hurt me. Perhaps she felt justified in the stance she took with me. Perhaps she truly just didn't understand the rules of the sales world.

After that epiphany, everything changed for the better for me. I would never allow myself to hold on to any negative feelings about someone because I knew that it was just me hurting myself. I'm so grateful that I learned this lesson very early on in my life because I was faced with a whopper of a situation to deal with a few years later.

It's About You, Not Them

Well into my adulthood, I received an email from my mother with one of the most vicious messages she had ever written me. In it she said some truly horrifying things. That letter was like a knife to the chest. It really rocked my world that day. I really felt like she was trying to annihilate me. I let myself feel all the emotion of that attack. I cried—no, I wailed—probably more so than I ever had during the time I'd lived with her in my early teens. I also felt like she was trying to goad me into some kind of a response—as if she was probing me to try to get a negative reaction out of me and make me play her same game.

But I had chosen in life not to let others suck me into their behavior patterns. I simply don't engage.

After letting myself feel the hurt and pain from that letter and allowing space so the emotions would subside, I felt a bit of relief knowing that she just helped me make a life changing decision: I eliminated her from my life. I protected my boundaries and preserved my personal power. And I did all this while forgiving her. Around the same time, she also wreaked havoc on the lives of some of my other relatives. She had to be suffering in big ways not to be able to have any kind of normal connection with any of the family members in her life. With that perspective, how could I not forgive her? I figured she must be dealing with a whole lot of inner conflict and negativity to lash out at others like that. She was the one who was really suffering and missing out on what could have been the most loving, supportive relationships in her life.

But just because I chose to forgive my mother doesn't mean that I have to choose to allow her into my life anymore. She wasn't capable of being anyone other than who she was, and I had to accept that.

In *Buddha's Brain*, Rich Hanson and Richard Mendius teach an exercise called Ten Thousand Things.[4] It is used to help broaden our perspective by putting ourselves in another person's shoes and analyzing what could be influencing their actions. When using it with my mother, here is how it played out. I asked myself if there were "ten thousand different things" that could have led my mother to write me such an email.

I considered the realities of her life such as her responsibilities, daily stress, personal demons, and so on. I had to ask myself if I knew much about my mother's childhood. Did she have a secret trauma I don't know about or that nobody knows? Did she grow up in an era where mental health was not acknowledged or understood? When she was younger, was she unable to get the help she might have gotten if she were coming of age today? I had to consider how my mother processed conversations, criticisms, and daily interactions. Being a very creative person, could my mother's eccentricities have been a detriment to her personality in how she relates to others? Could it be a DNA thing?

The point is that considering the plethora of things that informs (or doesn't inform) a person helps you let go of your own perceptions and become more objective. You realize none of it is about you. This exercise is an act of compassion, even empathy.

After I made the commitment to myself, I let my mother go from my life. And it didn't require me reacting or responding in any way. It just was. My physical body felt energetic and vibrant after this work was done, and that energy alone told me my choice was right. Choosing not to allow my mother into my life anymore felt good. And feeling good is a primary objective of mine in life. I no longer give her the prime real estate in my brain. I've never reached out to her, and she's never reached out to me since she wrote that letter. I continue to feel healthy and positive about my decision, more than fifteen years later.

Responding with Forgiveness

In the previous chapter, I talk about the need to learn how to respond thoughtfully rather than react mindlessly. If I had fired back a reactionary email to my mother, who hurt me so deeply, I wouldn't have had the wherewithal to respond by reflecting in the way that I did. In that reflection I observed why I was hurt and what my mother's Ten Thousand Things might have been. I was able to come to a rational, well-informed, and thoughtfully considered decision: not to have her in my life.

Reacting in the way that I think she wanted me to—shooting back blame and name calling, ranting on the phone—would have kept me in a spiral of pain, anger, and shame, and I don't think I would be the same person today if I had done that.

I chose to respond with forgiveness and let go of the anger and hurt I'd carried around for so long. Being aware of what the impact was on *me*, I was able to practice the self-love of healing rather than surrender to the immediate gratification of retaliation.

JOURNALING SUGGESTION

What Anger Are You Holding On To?

- Reflect on and write down situations in which you felt anger or resentment toward someone that you're still holding on to.
- How has your resentment affected you personally? Is your negative thinking creating negative energy in your life?
- What might happen if you were to let go of that resentment and enter a state of forgiveness?

Chapter 26

Create a Self-Love Loop

A loop is a structure, series, or process, the end of which is connected to the beginning. You probably have heard the term feedback loop, which is important because feedback loops allow living organisms to maintain homeostasis. Homeostasis enables us to keep our internal environment relatively constant—not too hot, or too cold, not too hungry or tired. This regulation system is healthy and ongoing.

Just like with feedback loops, I believe we can strengthen our internal mechanism for regulating self-love to create a self-love loop that is strong and infinite. One of the ways I do this is to celebrate small wins as I achieve them. As briefly mentioned earlier, we tend to downplay our achievements, choosing not to recognize when we have provided value to the world, while we overplay our struggles, defects, or mistakes. Our losses cause much more pain than our wins cause happiness. This is due to *loss aversion*, which psychologists describe as a bias that we humans have that makes the pain of losing psychologically twice as powerful as the pleasure of gaining. What a bad habit, and a hard one to break, but not an impossible one! We need to focus on incremental success and celebrate each win no matter how big or small.

Set Doable Goals, Celebrate Small Victories

The old adage about taking baby steps couldn't be more true, especially when it comes to goal setting. It's all about taking constant, small steps toward your goals. Even something as simple as daily journaling is progress. Or applying for a loan, saving money from your paycheck, going for a walk if you're trying to work out more—everything you do to work toward your goals counts, and keeping up the progress every day keeps the momentum going. And it just plain feels good. You get an extra energy surge for the day just knowing that you made progress.

During a University of Texas commencement speech, Admiral William McRaven said, "If you make your bed every morning, you will have accomplished the first task of the day. It will give you a small sense of pride, and it will encourage you to do another task, and another. . . . And [soon] that one task completed will have turned into many tasks completed."[1] He also pointed out that even if you have a bad day, being able to come home to a bed that was made by you helps provide a sense of accomplishment that encourages you to do better the next day.

Setting goals that are doable and then acknowledging that we saw them to completion is one of the ways the self-love loop stays taut. Sometimes we find ourselves procrastinating on the things that we'd like to accomplish. But when we make it a priority to accomplish a personal goal, we are telling ourselves that we are important. Committing to ourselves means committing to our goals.

Most of the time, we don't accomplish a goal because we made it too lofty, or we are striving only for perfection. If you would like to lose weight, don't set the goal at forty pounds; set the goal at drinking more water that week or eliminating one sugary treat a day. You will succeed more often, giving you a sense of accomplishment, just like the admiral says about making the bed. When we succeed we feel good and want to continue.

London-based performance psychologist James King suggests that in addition to setting goals that are achievable, we should be sure the goals we set are within what he calls our "sweet spot."[2] Have you ever watched *American Idol* auditions, where on occasion, one of the judges will ask the contestant to repeat the song but in a different key? Suddenly, their perfectly fine singing voice transforms to give the audience chills. They just needed to switch to a key that was concordant with their skill set and vice versa. Setting concordant goals that lie in our sweet spot is sort of like that.

One of the ways to kill our self-love loop is demotivation, which happens when we can't see that we are making progress and winning the day, every day. This is why it's important to acknowledge and celebrate small victories. Motivation is the driver that keeps us on the path to what we want, so when we diminish our victories, we diminish our motivation. "Demotivation usually comes because we are unsure of how far we are to our goals," writes Jenny Marchal for *Lifehack*. "We sometimes blindly believe that the goal is still so far away when it could actually be just around the corner—something we will never know if we give up."[3]

Acknowledging the proactive things we do (like making the bed) rewards the circuitry of our brains, which releases chemicals that produce pride and confidence and compels us to go further toward our next achievement.

Silencing the Inner Critic

I remember recently playing a tennis match. It was a competitive league game, and it was by far the most intensely challenging game I can ever remember playing with an opponent who was quite evenly matched with me. Each game went to deuce (a tie) more than once. So each game would end up lasting five to ten minutes. We both made very few mistakes in the games, so it took many volleys for one of us to hit the ball out.

By the time our two-hour court reservation had expired, we hadn't even wrapped up our second set. As such, we had to find new courts to move to since all the courts where we had been playing were fully booked. Luckily, we found some public courts that were open nearby. So we picked up the set where we left off. I had won the first set; now my opponent won the second set. This meant that after playing for three hours at this point, we were moving into a third set to determine the match winner.

We had started playing at 9:00 a.m. By the time our third match started, it was in the full heat of the day at around 85 degrees. I hadn't brought enough snacks or water to hold me over for such a long, strenuous game. Thankfully, my opponent's boyfriend had extra water that he was happy to share. I mustered up as much inner strength to give my best in this third set. But a quarter of the way in, I was losing steam quickly. While I was exhausted physically, it was the mental steam that I was quickly losing. Admittedly, I had also drunk a bit too much wine the night before, which I knew was not a smart thing to do before a game.

That little voice, my inner critic, started popping up in my head telling me I should just let her win the game so that my physical beating would stop. It was so brutal out there in the heat, and I felt absolutely exhausted. But then I'd make a great point and then another. Rather than listen to that voice telling me to quit, I embraced my inner warrior goddess—or IWG, as I call her (more in the next chapter)—and started encouraging myself, patting myself on the back for having made such a great point and having great hustle in getting to the ball. I noticed how it shifted my energy. I went from wanting to quit to feeling like I could win. I kept it up through most of the third set.

I could easily have listened to the self-defeating voice that would have dictated my eventual defeat. Instead, I felt encouraged and empowered to try my best, point-by-point. I went on to win by just two games after a grueling four-and-a-half-hour match.

It's so important to pat yourself on the back and encourage yourself. By doing this, it allows you to empower yourself without relying on outside sources for encouragement. It's like having your own cheer-leading squad anytime you need it. And it all comes from within you. It may sound cheesy, but trust me, it feels awesome when you do it. So go ahead and give it a try next time when you do something you're proud of.

Unfortunately, our inner critic tends to get a pretty big stage in our lives. It's loud and ugly, and for some reason, we've let it become the main voice we listen to. We just let it run wild and let it tell us all kinds of terrible things about ourselves that just aren't true. Then we make the choice to believe those things that it tells us. We believe these false things to be true because we choose to make some kind of identification with this inner critic as if it's ourselves. But it's not us. It's not who we truly are.

It says things like, "Who are you to go for that job? You're not fully qualified!" It says, "No one cares what you have to say. You don't matter, so don't even bother speaking up." It says, "You're ugly," "You're fat," "You are never going to achieve anything great in life because you were raised poor or without the same opportunities as others, you don't have the right education to get anywhere, you have just have bad luck in life."

Your inner critic is based on fear and insecurities. It holds us back from making bold choices based on what we really want. It's very easy just to listen to the inner critic and stay where it's safe—safe in fear, because it's what we know.

We can choose to listen to that voice, or we can choose to foster the IWG instead. Our inner warrior goddess observes when this inner critic is telling us something negative. She steps in and says, "I can choose to listen to you, or I can choose to look at the opposite of what you are telling me and see if there might be truth there for me instead."

What can I do instead to encourage myself right now when my inner critic wants to bring me down? I can look for truths within that I know about myself and build those truths up instead. Even better, my IWG becomes the first and only presence that comes up in the first place.

When you start to let her come out and encourage and pat yourself on the back regularly, pretty soon your relationship with her grows strong in your life. She becomes your new best friend. And guess what? Your inner critic makes fewer appearances because she starts to realize you aren't listening to her anymore anyway.

Be Your Own Cheerleader

Not only is it okay to pat yourself on the back when you accomplish something, but cheering yourself on with kind, motivating, congratulatory words is vital to live life to your fullest potential. Your wins are part of your story—and remember, we want to own our story. The opposite of this concept is probably what most of us battle with: our inner critic. Our inner critic is that little voice telling you that you're not qualified to get that promotion, you're an imposter—who are you to start that business; you aren't pretty enough to get a guy like that; if you confront that person with how you feel, they will react terribly; you're not qualified to write that book.

Unfortunately, this inner critic does a great job of convincing us that what it says is true. But ultimately, we control what we choose to believe. As I sit here and type these words, I am patting myself on the back for kicking butt today with the number of words I have gotten on the page. It feels great when I congratulate myself for my efforts. It lifts my soul and keeps me in the game!

Words can have the same kind of placebo effect as pills. People who've been told by others that they are attractive, successful, or doing a great job feel like what is said is true. And if they can feel those things are true, they tend to embody those traits. But did you know that you can provide yourself with those same words of encouragement and it will have the same affect?

Just like buying myself a ring feels better than receiving jewelry from someone else, praising myself feels better than when someone else praises me. I learned that it's much better to care about how I feel about myself than about what anyone else thinks. So when I'm impressing myself, I need to give myself those well-deserved kudos.

Giving Yourself a High-Five

- How do you feel about the idea of patting yourself on the back on a regular basis?
- What are some small things that you accomplished in the past week that you can acknowledge and give yourself a high-five for?
- Where do you currently look to receive your kudos from?

Chapter 27

Embrace Your Inner Warrior Goddess (Notorious IWG)

Now you have to make a big choice. Love, happiness, and success are the best feelings in life. These are the things we desperately crave. Isn't that why we work so hard at our jobs, get involved in relationships, own pets, seek hobbies, take care of our health, and have children? We do these things ultimately to have a good life and feel whole. But the truth is, real wholeness can only come when we love ourselves and take care of ourselves. We can, of course, love our job, but the job cannot give us love. We can love our partner, but they cannot be responsible for making us happy or even loving us the way we can love ourselves. We can love our kids, but we cannot make them responsible for our life purpose.

Real wholeness can only come when we love ourselves and take care of ourselves.

No one else can or should be responsible for our happiness. Imagine the pressure you would feel, and the energy it would suck out of you, if someone expected you to be responsible for making them happy? Not only is it not realistic, but expectations are burdens we put on other people. And no one—not Superman, not Oprah, not the Dalai Lama—could provide you with same joy that can only come from within.

When we accept ourselves, the true stories of our lives, and stop the shame we let bind us to the unhappiness we feel in the present, our lives become rich. The hole that shame has burned into our soul is filled and we become whole. True happiness comes from living with purpose, pursuing our passions and hobbies, taking care of our health and well-being, knowing our worth, loving ourselves for everything that we are—flaws and all! Now how can anyone, or any external source, possibly make us happy the same way we can make ourselves happy? Happiness is a commitment to oneself, not putting the onus on others to commit to us. To own your story means you learn to commit to yourself.

I've come to describe my self-love journey as embracing my *inner warrior goddess*. She's still me, but she is the part of me that is the epitome of all my self-love. I find it helpful to envision her, especially during times that challenge me and my commitment to my self-love journey. This inspired me to cofound TigerFeather, a company that produces apparel and other products that serve to symbolize and honor our Notorious IWG and all that she stands for.

- She's the fearless protector of her energy.
- She says no when she feels like saying no.
- She has zero reservations about recognizing and setting her boundaries.
- She knows her worth and values herself. She never lets anyone try to devalue her.
- She looks out for red flags with potential partners and has absolutely no problem moving on if something doesn't seem quite right.
- She isn't focused just on pleasing others without ensuring that she is also pleasing herself—every single day.

- She communicates her needs.
- She takes space when she needs it.
- She doesn't look to others for any kind of validation. As long as she is happy with herself and her life, that's all that matters. She knows not everyone will like her. She knows it's not a reflection of her, as she doesn't like everyone herself—and that's okay.
- She embraces her inner cheerleader and tells her inner critic to take a hike.
- She focuses on what makes her feel good and makes it a priority, no matter what.
- If something or someone is making her feel bad, or even just not good, she recognizes that as her cue to stand up and fight for herself. Yes, it's a battle. But that's okay because she is a warrior, ready to fight for herself. No one else is going to. It's her responsibility.
- She makes sure she tries to spend time in silence, in nature, or journaling every day, tuning in to her spirit and connecting with her higher power.
- She cares about her health and fitness. She takes care of herself, and that makes her feel good. She does it for herself, not for any external validation.
- She is financially independent and sets herself up to never have to have money as an unnecessary stress in her life.
- She is compassionate with herself.
- She forgives others. She doesn't hold on to anger and resentment, as she knows the only person anger and resentment hurts is herself.
- She says goodbye to toxic relationships forever. She says hello to relationships she chooses consciously.
- She knows she doesn't owe anyone anything other than to herself.
- She doesn't allow people in her life who bring her down and don't lift her up.

- She understands that because of old conditioning beyond her control, her energy will be pulled away by others; she may want to naturally let that happen. But she is able to step back and recognize when this is happening simply by recognizing when she isn't feeling good or happy. She forgives herself because it's not her fault, though it's really hard to fight this natural tendency. But when she recognizes it, she doesn't blame anyone, including herself. She just gets right back into her self-care routine.
- She remembers that good enough is good enough.

Your inner warrior goddess has always been a part of you. She's sitting there waiting for you to embrace her and make her a bigger part of your life. Let's fill the world with a new breed of warrior goddesses and watch our planet become a better place for all.

Acknowledgments

Thank you, Marion, for showing me what unwavering, unconditional love is and for being my rock. I don't even want to think about what life would have been like for me without you as my grandmother.

Vincent, you've had so many hurdles to overcome in your young life. Thank you, my son, for your bravery and willingness to be vulnerable by allowing me to share your story with others.

To my amazing friends, thank you for always being there to love and support me on my journey. I love and appreciate you all so very much.

To my family, thank you for being my cheerleaders throughout this process.

Thank you to all the wonderful folks I've met along my path since I first decided to write this book. Whether we met through our networking groups, social media, interviews, mutual friends, or acquaintances, your support and encouragement have been such a blessing. Thank you for showing me what it's like to really feel like we are all connected as one.

To Michele Matrisciani, a big thank-you for believing in me, my mission, and this book's concept and for helping me edit and develop it. It was a pleasure and an honor to work with you every step of the way. Thank you to the entire team at Greenleaf Book Group for helping me polish my manuscript and design and bring *I Love Me More* to market. Being a first-time author, I really appreciate how you made the entire publication process so smooth, professional, and easy.

Thank you, Sherry Deutschmann, and the entire team and community at BrainTrust for believing in me and supporting this book. I feel incredibly honored to be the inaugural author for the BrainTrust

Ink imprint, a collaboration with Greenleaf Book Group. I appreciate the opportunity to be a part of this initiative to make a positive impact in the world as it relates to our common goal of bringing about social equality and women's empowerment.

Thank you, Geoff Galloway, for not only acquiring my company but being such an incredible believer and supporter of this book and of my mission. Your integrity, your goodwill, and the examples you set as a businessman, father, and husband are beyond heartwarming.

Thank you to all the current friends, former friends, relatives, and past partners who played a role in my life and, subsequently, in this book. Each and every one of you not only served as my teacher, allowing me to grow in my own personal development, but now also serve to help others on their journeys.

And finally, thank you to the universe for giving me the opportunity to create this book and connect and share with others in ways I had never previously imagined. I'm so grateful for the unlimited possibilities that exist in this world when we accept our roles as cocreators and free ourselves to imagine, feel worthy, and move into inspired action.

Notes

Chapter 2

1. *Lexico English Dictionary*, s.v. "self-love," https://www.lexico.com/en/definition/self-love (accessed August 12, 2021).

2. Jeffrey Borenstein, "Self-Love and What It Means," Brain & Behavior Research Foundation, February 12, 2020, https://www.bbrfoundation.org/blog/self-love-and-what-it-means.

3. Borenstein, "Self-Love and What It Means."

4. Elyse Santilli, "15 Truths about Self Love We All Need to Remember," https://elysesantilli.com/truths-about-self-love/ (accessed August 12, 2021).

5. Vanessa Scotto, "The Difference between Selfishness and Self-Love," *Yinova* (blog), https://www.yinovacenter.com/blog/the-difference-between-selfishness-and-self-love/ (accessed July 22, 2021).

6. Quoted in Tara Parker-Pope, "Go Easy on Yourself, a New Wave of Research Urges," *New York Times*, February 28, 2011, http://well.blogs.nytimes.com/2011/02/28/go-easy-on-yourself-a-new-wave-of-research-urges/.

Chapter 3

1. Tara Parker-Pope, "Go Easy on Yourself, a New Wave of Research Urges," *New York Times*, February 28, 2011, https://well.blogs.nytimes.com/2011/02/28/go-easy-on-yourself-a-new-wave-of-research-urges/.

2. University of Exeter, "Being Kind to Yourself Has Mental and Physical Benefits," *ScienceDaily*, February 6, 2019, https://www.sciencedaily.com/releases/2019/02/190206200344.htm.

3. University of Exeter, "Being Kind to Yourself."

4. Rebecca A. Clay, "Don't Cry over Spilled Milk—the Research on Why It's Important to Give Yourself a Break," American Psychological Association, September 2016, https://www.apa.org/monitor/2016/09/ce-corner.

5. Joanna Nolan, "Self-Love in Recovery: Simple Steps Are Often the Most Power-ful," Eating Recovery Center, February 27, 2019, https://www.eatingrecoverycenter .com/blog/self-care/self-love-in-recovery-simple-steps-often-most-powerful.

6. Anita Moorjani, *Dying to Be Me: My Journey from Cancer, to Near Death, to True Healing* (Carlsbad, CA: Hay House, 2012), 165.

7. Eckhart Tolle, *The Power of Now* (Novato, CA: Namaste, 2004), 114.

Chapter 4

1. Quoted in Melissa Moore and Michele Matrisciani, *Whole: How I Learned to Fill the Fragments of My Life with Forgiveness, Hope, Strength, and Creativity* (New York: Rodale Books, 2016), 191.

2. Quoted in Moore and Matrisciani, *Whole*, 191.

3. Moore and Matrisciani, *Whole*, 192.

4. Cecilia Meis, "Gabby Bernstein Shows You How to Love Yourself First," *Success*, January 1, 2018, https://www.success.com/gabby-bernstein-shows-you-how -to-love-yourself-first/.

Chapter 5

1. Deepak Chopra, *The Seven Spiritual Laws of Success* (San Rafael, CA: Amber-Allen and New World Library, 1994), 10–11.

2. Chopra, *The Seven Spiritual Laws of Success*, 12.

3. Chopra, *The Seven Spiritual Laws of Success*, 11.

Chapter 6

1. Don Miguel Ruiz, *The Four Agreements* (San Rafael, CA: Amber-Allen, 2011), 7.

2. Ruiz, *The Four Agreements*, 7.

3. Ruiz, *The Four Agreements*, 9.

4. Ruiz, The Four Agreements, 10.

5. Deepak Chopra, "The Hidden Cost of Judgement," LinkedIn, October 24, 2018, https://www.linkedin.com/pulse/hidden-cost-judgment-deepak-chopra -md-official.

6. Anita Moorjani, *Dying to Be Me: My Journey from Cancer, to Near Death, to True Healing* (Carlsbad, CA: Hay House, 2012), 139.

Chapter 7

1. Nadine Macaluso, Instagram post, July 2, 2021, https://www.instagram.com/p/CQ0vMA_NkJg/.

Chapter 9

1. Malcolm Gladwell, *Blink: The Power of Thinking without Thinking* (New York: Little, Brown, 2005), 10.
2. Gladwell, *Blink*, 11–12.
3. Gladwell, *Blink*, 15.

Chapter 12

1. Roy T. Bennett, *The Light in the Heart* (Self-published, 2020).
2. Laura Delarato, "What Happened When I Put Myself First In Every Situation," *NBC News*, February 17, 2018, https://www.nbcnews.com/better/health/what-happened-when-i-put-myself-first-every-situation-ncna815746.
3. Delarato, "What Happened."

Chapter 13

1. Elizabeth Gilbert, "Confessions of an Over-giver," *Oprah.com*, https://www.oprah.com/spirit/how-to-avoid-giving-too-much-of-yourself-elizabeth-gilbert (accessed July 22, 2021).
2. Quoted in Kristine Fellizar, "7 Signs You're Giving Too Much of Yourself in Your Relationship," *Bustle*, May 1, 2019, https://www.bustle.com/p/7-signs-youre-giving-too-much-of-yourself-in-your-relationship-17292805.
3. Fellizar, "7 Signs."
4. Iyanla Vanzant, "Why You Should Put Yourself First," *Oprah's LifeClass*, season 2, episode 201, March 26, 2012, https://www.oprah.com/oprahs-lifeclass/why-you-should-put-yourself-first-video.

Chapter 14

1. Quoted in Lisa Ryan, "A Relationship Expert Reveals the 3 Signs Your New Relationship Will Last," *Business Insider*, June 23, 2016, https://www.businessinsider.com/a-relationship-expert-reveals-the-3-signs-your-new-relationship-will-last-2016-6.
2. Stan Kapuchinski, *Say Goodbye to Your PDI (Personality Disordered Individual): Recognize People Who Make You Miserable and Eliminate Them from Your Life for Good!* (Deerfield Beach, FL: Heath Communications, 2007), 10.

Chapter 15

1. Henry Cloud and John Townsend, *Boundaries: When to Say Yes, How to Say No to Take Control of Your Life* (Philadelphia, PA: Running Press, 2004).
2. Allen Cheng, "Boundaries Book Summary," https://www.allencheng.com/boundaries-book-summary-henry-cloud-john-townsend/ (accessed July 23, 2021).
3. Iyanla Vanzant, "Why You Should Put Yourself First," *Oprah's LifeClass*, season 2, episode 201, March 26, 2012, https://www.oprah.com/oprahs-lifeclass/why-you-should-put-yourself-first-video.
4. Cloud and Townsend, *Boundaries*.

Chapter 16

1. *Lexico English Dictionary*, s.v. "shame," https://www.lexico.com/en/definition/shame (accessed August 12, 2021).
2. Nadine Macaluso, "The Relationship between Shame and Complex PTSD," *Dr. Nae* (blog), https://www.nadinemacaluso.com/the-relationship-between-shame-and-complex-ptsd/ (accessed July 23, 2021).
3. Marianne Williamson, *A Return to Love: Reflections on the Principles of "A Course in Miracles"* (New York: Harper Collins, 2009), 13.
4. Macaluso, "The Relationship between Shame and Complex PTSD."
5. Brianna Johnson, "Are You a Chronic Self-Abandoner?" National Alliance on Mental Illness, April 30, 2018, https://www.nami.org/Blogs/NAMI-Blog/April-2018/Are-You-a-Chronic-Self-Abandoner.
6. Macaluso, "The Relationship between Shame and Complex PTSD."
7. Macaluso, "The Relationship between Shame and Complex PTSD."
8. Bret Lyon, "Shame and Trauma," Center for Healing Shame, August 21, 2017, https://healingshame.com/articles/2017/8/21/shame-and-trauma.
9. Lyon, "Shame and Trauma."

Chapter 17

1. Stephanie Ritz, "Tips for Women to Get Ahead at Work," *Jenna Banks Show,* July 10, 2021, https://www.youtube.com/watch?v=8dAClXZ5vvA&t=22s.

2. Christina Pazzanese, "Women Less Inclined to Self-Promote Than Men, Even for a Job," *Harvard Gazette,* February 7, 2020, https://news.harvard.edu/gazette/ story/2020/02/men-better-than-women-at-self-promotion-on-job-leading-to -inequities/.

3. Lois P. Frankel, *Nice Girls Don't Get the Corner Office* (New York: Grand Central, 2014), 119.

4. Linda Babcock, Maria Recalde, Lise Vesterlund, and Laurie Weingart, "Gender Differences in Accepting and Receiving Requests for Tasks with Low Promotability," *American Economic Review* 107, no. 3 (2017), https://www.aeaweb.org/ articles?id=10.1257/aer.20141734.

5. Bryan Robinson, "How Self-Love Boosts Job Performance and Career Success," *Forbes,* February 5, 2021, https://www.forbes.com/sites/bryanrobinson/ 2021/02/05/how-self-love-boosts-job-performance-and-career-success/ ?sh=6885356a30c1.

6. Pema Chödrön, *When Things Fall Apart* (Boulder, CO: Shambhala, 2005), 3.

Chapter 18

1. Capital One, "Mind over Money Study: Getting in the Right Money Mindset," January 26, 2020, https://www.capitalone.com/about/ newsroom/2020-capitalone-mindovermoneystudytips/.

2. Emma Edwards, "7 Ways a Lack of Self Love Could Be Ruining Your Finances," *Broke Generation,* June 11, 2020, https://thebrokegeneration.com/ blog/2020/06/11/self-love-finances/.

3. Suze Orman, "What Parents Get So Wrong about College," *LinkedIn,* January 23, 2020, https://www.linkedin.com/pulse/what-parents-get-so-wrong-college -suze-orman.

Part V

1. Family Caregiver Alliance, "Caregiving," 2009, https://www.caregiver.org/ resource/caregiving/.

Chapter 19

1. Claire Samuels, "What Is the Sandwich Generation? Unique Stress and Responsibilities for Caregivers between Generations," A Place for Mom, July 7, 2020, https://www.aplaceformom.com/caregiver-resources/articles/what-is-the-sandwich-generation.
2. Samuels, "What Is the Sandwich Generation?"

Chapter 20

1. Shelly Stasney, "5 Steps to Self-Love: An Essential Component to Parenting," *This-n-That Parenting*, February 27, 2018, https://www.thisnthatparenting.com/the-most-important-thing-to-do-when-becoming-parents/.
2. Jennifer Kimmelman, "10 Life Changing Tips by Deepak Chopra," Madison Marriage and Family Therapy, June 2, 2015, http://www.madisonmft.com/articles/2015/6/02/10-life-changing-tips-by-deepak-chopra.
3. Kahlil Gibran, *The Prophet*, 2nd ed. (London: William Heinemann, 1926), 21.
4. Marvin G. Knittel, "When Is It Time to Let Go of Our Young Adult Child?" *Psychology Today*, March 20, 2018, https://www.psychologytoday.com/us/blog/how-help-friend/201803/when-is-it-time-let-go-our-young-adult-child.
5. Susan Roulusonis Pione, "Self Love vs. Parenting: It's Not One or the Other," TUT, April 27, 2016, https://www.tut.com/287-self-love-vs-parenting-its-not-one-or-the-other/.
6. Pione, "Self Love vs. Parenting."

Part VI

1. *Sex and the City* (New Line Cinema, 2008).

Chapter 21

1. Deepak Chopra, *The Seven Spiritual Laws of Success* (San Rafael, CA: Amber-Allen and New World Library, 1994), 70.
2. Marianne Williamson, *A Return to Love: Reflections on the Principles of "A Course in Miracles"* (San Francisco, CA: HarperOne, 1996), 190.

Chapter 22

1. "Sacred Symbols for Personal Power," Spirit of Water, https://thespiritofwater
   .com/pages/sacred-symbols-for-personal-power (accessed July 23, 2021).
2. Brené Brown, *Daring Greatly: How the Courage to Be Vulnerable Transforms the Way
   We Live, Love, Parent, and Lead* (New York: Penguin, 2015), 129.
3. Brown, *Daring Greatly*, 130.
4. Brown, *Daring Greatly*, 130.

Chapter 23

1. Tony Robbins, "Are You with the Right Person?" *Tony Robbins Podcast*, September
   3, 2019, https://www.youtube.com/watch?v=dC50dYcMPF4.
2. Joseph Campbell, *A Joseph Campbell Companion: Reflections on the Art of Living*
   (New York: HarperCollins, 1991), 48.
3. Quoted in Brittany Wong, "How to Politely Tell Your S.O. That You Just Need to
   Be Left Alone," *HuffPost*, February 13, 2020, https://www.huffpost.com/entry/
   needing-to-be-alone-in-relationship_l_5e444518c5b61f8ad4e302e8.

Chapter 24

1. Melissa Eisler, "Respond vs. React: How to Keep Your Cool in Times of Stress,"
   Melissa Eisler, July 13, 2018, https://melissaeisler.com/respond-vs-react-how-to
   -keep-your-cool-in-times-of-stress/.
2. Eisler, "Respond vs. React."

Chapter 25

1. Melissa Moore and Michele Matrisciani, *Whole: How I Learned to Fill the Fragments of My Life with Forgiveness, Hope, Strength, and Creativity* (New York: Rodale
   Books, 2016), 63.
2. Fred Luskin, *Forgive for Good: A Proven Prescription for Health and Happiness* (San
   Francisco: HarperOne, 2010).
3. Quoted in Moore and Matrisciani, *Whole*, 63.
4. Rich Hanson and Richard Mendius, *Buddha's Brain* (Oakland, CA: New Harbin-
   ger, 2009).

Chapter 26

1. William McRaven, University of Texas commencement speech, Austin, TX, May 19, 2014.

2. James A. King, *Accelerating Excellence: The Principles That Drive Elite Performance* (James King, 2021), 35.

3. Jenny Marchal, "How to Celebrate Small Wins to Achieve Big Goals," *Lifehack*, May 16, 2021, https://www.lifehack.org/396379/how-celebrate-small-wins -achieve-big-goals.

About the Author

JENNA BANKS is an entrepreneur, public speaker, author, podcast host, real-estate investor, and self-love advocate. Having survived a traumatic upbringing, as well as a nearly fatal suicide attempt, she was able to thrive in the business world, despite being armed with only a high school equivalency diploma.

Early in her career, she worked in management and entrepreneurial roles, producing marketing products for major movie studios in Los Angeles, including Sony Pictures Entertainment, Paramount Pictures, and Warner Bros. She has also worked in the toy and games industry, including with well-known brands such as Hasbro, Mattel, and Lego.

As someone who learned to never question her instincts, she trusted the inner call to quit her comfortable six-figure corporate job and start a home-based marketing products business in 2012 with $400 and a laptop. While running the company, she simultaneously ramped up a profitable real-estate venture and then later sold her marketing products business for $500,000.

Since selling her company, she's now focused on what she feels is her higher purpose: to share her story and her message of empowerment and the incredible importance of self-love with the world through her writing; speaking engagements; *The Jenna Banks Show*, a podcast and video series; and her newest lifestyle brand, TigerFeather. When she's not working, Jenna enjoys collecting fine art, playing tennis, traveling, spending time with friends and family, and connecting with and inspiring other women to succeed and be empowered.

To receive inspiration and reminders from Jenna to help you on your self-love journey, sign up for her email list at www.jenna-banks.com or connect with her (@jennabanks.0) on Instagram or Facebook.